At Heaven's Gate

At Heaven's Gate

Gate

Reflections on Leading Worship

Richard Giles

CANTERBURY
PRESS
Norwich

First published in 2010 by the Canterbury Press Norwich
Editorial office
13–17 Long Lane,
London, EC1A 9PN, UK

Canterbury Press is an imprint of Hymns Ancient and
Modern Ltd (a registered charity)
13a Hellesdon Park Road, Norwich, Norfolk, NR6 5DR

www.scm-canterburypress.co.uk

British Library Cataloguing in Publication data

A catalogue record for this book is available
from the British Library

978-1-84825-046-8

Typeset by Regent Typesetting, London
Printed and bound in Great Britain by
CPI Bookmarque, Croydon

We do not have to die to arrive at the gates of Heaven. In fact, we have to be truly alive.

Thic Nhat Hanh, *Living Buddha, Living Christ*, p. 38

For Judy

(colleague and friend)

Contents

Preface

Mainstream churches and synagogues share the problem and promise of worship. If we do not meet the challenge of making prayer thrilling and authentic, we may well watch our constituencies wither. Whether conservative or liberal, the preponderance of Jews are simply bored in synagogue. Now, when many are wired to electronic instruments, sound bites are often the limit of the attention span.

No cleric can read this book without profit. Some will take it as a book of instruction, and use it as their guide. Others will extract from it, now one insight and now another. In our defensive posture, shepherds of all stripes of Judaism and Christianity will be enlightened.

We first met Richard Giles, my wife and I, when he applied his original ideas on sacred space to bring a new body and an exceptional spirit to the Episcopal Cathedral of Philadelphia where he served as Dean. When he disclosed his plan, I thought he was a prophet or a madman. When the Cathedral was dedicated, filled with the holy spirit, I knew he was a prophet.

A Hasidic leader told this parable. 'A man lost in a forest was relieved to find another person, and he asked for the way out. The other replied: "I can only tell you where not to go. Perhaps together we can find the way." We have tried many things to inspire our congregants without success. We need to journey together, and this book presents a path.

Ivan Caine
Rabbi of Society Hill Synagogue, Philadelphia, 1967–2001
Director of Biblical Studies, Reconstructionist Rabbinical College, Philadelphia, 1967–86

Introduction

Worship is a funny business, is it not? It can give our spirit wings to fly to the very gates of heaven, or it can drive us almost to despair. We can be entranced by worship, literally 'lost in wonder, love and praise', or driven to distraction by it, vowing to remain in bed on Sundays.

So getting worship right, or as right as we can, is of no little importance. Sadly, the prevailing pattern of worship in many mainstream churches indicates that we don't try very hard, or try for a while and give up, or try now and again before falling back into the same old routine.

'When all else has ceased, it will be worship which will remain.'[1] Thirty years have passed since Michael Marshall wrote these words in his seminal book *Renewal in Worship*, yet so little has changed that it is hard to suppress the unworthy thought that if all we are left with is worship as we know it, then heaven help us.

Despite the emergence of worship resources that previous generations could only have dreamt of, and technological developments that outpace us on every front, worship for many remains pedestrian and lifeless. It is too often dominated by people's instinctive resistance to change and even the superb new resources provided by the Church soon run into the sand if performed unimaginatively or sloppily for long enough.

---

1 Michael Marshall, *Renewal in Worship*, 1982, p. 23.

Worship continues to be largely experienced in a time warp; celebrated in rooms last rearranged when Queen Victoria was a girl, filled with the sound of music-making unchanged since we kicked Thomas Hardy's village orchestra into touch, reverberating with reassurances crafted in a time when every word of the Bible was believed to have been faxed directly from head office. Nostalgia and reassurance seem to be the hallmarks of much of what passes for worship. 'The world moves on but somehow time stands still. Welcome to the C of E.'[2]

No wonder then that worship for many is a duty rather than a joy, a comfortable gathering of the likeminded rather than a breathtaking encounter with the living God. We have all encountered worship leaders who plod their weary and uncertain way from one page to the next, careless of the treasures at their disposal, unmindful of the glory to be revealed in the gifts and ministries drawn forth from an expectant assembly engaged in an enterprise that straddles earth and heaven.

While we fiddle, Rome burns, and we have in the process lost generation after generation of thinking, engaged and spiritual people who see the Church as an utter irrelevance to contemporary life. Disengaged, repetitive worship has a great deal to do with this exodus and, despite glorious exceptions here and there, the local church resembles more and more a Sunday outing for the over fifties. Often there will be a sprinkling of young children wherever good work is being done in that department, but as soon as they grow out of it, a yawning gap is left where the 15–50-year-olds ought to be.

We need therefore to work hard at getting worship as right and as true as humanly possible, not as an aesthetic

---

2 Hugh Muir, *Guardian Diary*, 15 June 2010.

experience for our own benefit, but as a pathway home for all those bemused by our grasping and violent society, and who have looked for, but not yet found, meaning and community, direction and joy.

Anyone venturing to offer advice on worship embarks on a perilous exercise, and the most that can be hoped for in a little book like this is that it might serve merely as a gentle nudge in the right direction. Liturgical hackles rise quicker than any other, and (as those who wear a wedding ring will know) a kindly suggestion can easily be misinterpreted as an imperious directive.

Every community of faith is responsible under God for its own worship, and in the final analysis good worship is a vision caught rather than a formula taught. What follows is an attempt to share a few experiences of a journey in which worship has been a primary formative influence in my own spiritual life and in that of the communities I was privileged to serve. For us, as for countless others, worship formed the pavements and hedgerows defining our Damascus Road.

Above all it recalls us to the wonder of worship, and reminds us that when the people of God assemble to break open the word and to break bread, we are operating at two dimensions; gathered at a certain time and place, here and now, yet recognizing that when we do so we stand at the gate of heaven, handling holy things, and touching the eternal mystery.

PART I

Possibilities and Problems

When in the tenth century, Vladimir, Prince of Kiev, a pagan searching still for the meaning of life, sent his emissaries on a fact-finding tour across Europe in search of the true religion, they found that neither the Muslims of Bulgaria, nor the Christians of Rome, had anything to offer. Finally, arriving in Constantinople, they witnessed the Divine Liturgy in the great Church of the Holy Wisdom. Here they entered another plane, for they reported: 'We knew not whether we were in heaven or on earth, for surely there is no such splendour or beauty anywhere upon earth. We cannot describe it to you, only this we know, that God dwells there among men.'[3]

The goal

When we wonder why worship is so important that we should spend so much time and energy trying to get it right, and get so exasperated at those we think get it wrong, when we ask what all the fuss is about, this account of a tenth-century encounter with true worship reminds us of the purpose of it all. In worship we aspire to come to the very threshold of the heavenly places, willingly allowing

---

3 Kallistos Ware, *The Orthodox Church*, 1995, p. 269.

ourselves a moment of sensory confusion, not sure any more whether we are in heaven or on earth.

The challenge

The people of God deserve nothing less than worship that takes us to the threshold of heaven, and if this is not our experience, at least some of the time, something is badly amiss, and we shall need to start again.

In *The Looking Glass War* John le Carré describes the awful moment when, after months of preparation, the ideology of the secret service is called to account in the shape of a human being whose life they must now put at risk: 'But as he observed this man bobbing beside him, animate and quick, he recognized that hitherto they had courted ideas, incestuously among themselves; now they had a human being on their hands, and this was he.'[4]

Sunday worship for us should be the scary moment when we put all our praying, our Bible reading, our spiritual formation, and house group meetings to the test. After all this 'courting of ideas' we come to the crunch; has it all been for nothing, or will God actually show up at the rendezvous, as arranged? Worship challenges us by asking 'dare we risk it'?

John Betjeman's exquisite little poem 'In a Bath Teashop' takes us to a cosy setting differing wildly from le Carré's dramatic frontier, yet enshrines a truth equally as challenging. He describes in just four lines the experience of two very ordinary people, one of them a thorough rogue, who, enraptured by the love each has for the other, are so transformed that they become for a moment 'a little lower than the angels'.

---

4 John le Carré, *The Looking Glass War*, 1965, p. 156.

It could just as well have been titled 'In church on Sunday'. For how can it conceivably be that this odd collection of misfits we call 'church', meeting in a draughty building on a rainy Sunday in February, is in fact a community of transformation engaged in nothing less than making the presence of God real and tangible in time and space? But if we have eyes to see, that is exactly what confronts us.

In opening the door into the room where the assembly of God's people is ready and waiting to worship, we discover it to be nothing less than our own little tradesmen's entrance into the kingdom of God. Here in this unprepossessing corner of the world, as part of this group of very ordinary people, we stand at heaven's gate. When worship really takes hold of us, we shall have a hard time working out whether or not heaven has already begun.

What comes first?

One of the reasons that worship for us might be a little less sensational than that which blew away the tenth-century Russians is that we all too easily relegate worship from the premier to a lower division of activity in the church. When push comes to shove in this performance-centred culture of ours, worship doesn't appear to *do* anything.

It is a measure of the Church's loss of self-confidence that we ourselves have come to half believe that worship is an add-on to, not a prerequisite of, the full authentic Christian life. We find ourselves saying, 'once we have a decent mission statement, a shared ministry scheme, an outreach ministry, then we can turn our attention to worship'. This is the Christian Way put back-to-front.

If we really believe that the Sunday gathering of God's people is the sacrament of their transformation, that if we get worship right, those who participate in it will be radically changed by the experience, and energized to be different people, exercising ministries and roles unthinkable before, then we shall award worship first, second and third place in our agenda, knowing that all the rest will follow.

Beginning or end?

Probably no one is quite sure when diaries and calendars began to lay out each week with Monday as the first day of each week, and Sunday as the last. Whatever the timing, or the cause, the end result has been that our weekly worship is now seen by many as taking up a position at the back of the line, at the fag end of the week.

This is a far cry from the first Christians' weekly celebration of joyous thanksgiving and victory on the Lord's Day, the first day of the working week.[5] Because their celebration took place very early in the morning, before work began, the link with the resurrection was heightened, and each Lord's Day was a mini Easter.

No wonder our experience of Sunday worship is by comparison so often lacklustre. Not only are we operating on a day taken out of the working week (from 321 CE), it now feels like the last day rather than the first, a day for consuming the leftovers and tidying up before the real week begins.

Perhaps if we really meant business about re-energizing the people of God we should experiment with a new pattern of worship in which we boldly re-entered into the early Church's experience of gathering for weekly worship early on the first working day, giving over Sunday to

---

5 Matthew 28.1; 1 Corinthians 16.2.

4

enjoying a lie in, a late breakfast and the weekend papers with the best of them.

It would be interesting to see what happened in the first parish that advertised Mondays at 6 am as the main weekly gathering of its faith community. My guess is that (once the initial shrieks had died down), active membership would in time grow as worship was again experienced as the event which kick-starts our reimmersion in daily life. The direct links between worship and formation, and worship and social action, would have been restored.

Little things mean a lot

A sacramental approach – the insight that for all humankind (even those who reject or sideline sacraments with a capital 'S') actions speak louder than words – is part and parcel of daily life. We work best when we start with the particular and then move to the general. If we can once grasp hold of something manageable and tangible, we can in time move to the bigger picture. Such small signs – a bunch of flowers to say 'I love you' or 'sorry' for example – can in some inexplicable way convey truths or feelings or intentions quite beyond their physical properties.

Jesus took this natural human way of working to convey to his circle of close followers insights which lay beyond their comprehension or imagining. The Gospels' account of his life and teaching is permeated by his use of outward, visible and tangible signs – water, wine, bread, oil, even spittle – to convey his purpose and meaning. Starting with the familiar, he took them further, pointing to the mystery which lay beyond, which would otherwise have remained inaccessible and unknowable.

The same insight is essential to good worship. A sacramental approach is however a dynamic not static reality.

Never mind arguing over how many sacraments of the Church there are; instead let us recognize that the flow of God's love through outward signs and symbols, gestures and movement, is inexhaustible and ever present.

It is precisely for this reason that we need to begin here, with the small detail of the character and style and setting of our weekly gathering. It actually does matter if the altar cloth is hanging skew-whiff off the table, if one end of the president's stole is dragging on the floor, if the server's alb only reaches just below the knee, or if trainers are the only footwear on show.

Indifference to such detail indicates not only carelessness or insensitivity, but deep down a lack of conviction that worship is important and our participation in it a supreme privilege. We need to give it our very best, down to the smallest detail. Every action and gesture should count, for actions do speak louder than words, and sloppiness in the way we do worship will shout louder than any number of sermons proclaiming worship's theoretical importance.

The pastor

As long ago as the fourteenth century, Geoffrey Chaucer recognized clergy leadership as the key question.[6] With the best will in the world, it is extremely hard for a congregation to keep going if their leader has lost the plot. Although good worship does not depend on the ordained leader alone, it is difficult to sustain without her full, active and informed participation.

---

6 That if gold rust what shall iron do?
  For if a priest be foul, in whom we trust,
  No wonder is a lewd man to rust.
  Geoffrey Chaucer, 'The Parson's Tale', *The Canterbury Tales*

This, surprisingly, cannot be taken for granted, due mainly to the inadequacies of clergy training. First, deficient training can plant in the minds of clergy a fatal misunderstanding of worship as an academic subject, not a life-changing force.

Some imagine that because they once passed an exam called 'liturgy' there is nothing further to learn. Invitations to in-service training days on worship fall on deaf ears. Worship is not a particular pressure or burden – after a while you can do it on automatic – so brushing up on new ideas can always be left to next year.

Second, the pastor's role as educator and prophet is insufficiently understood. Surprise, surprise, the pastor is actually placed there to make something happen!

When working recently with a group of those about to be ordained, I ventured to suggest that they were to be sent forth as agents of transformation, managers of the process of change. Although some in the room evidently could not wait to get out there on the front line, the eyes of the majority glazed over; they simply switched off. They had managed to reach the eve of their ordination, their release into the bloodstream of the Church, with no inkling that they might ever be called upon to *change* anything.

How exactly we are to go about creating the culture in which change happens is of course a subject in its own right. It requires compassion and firmness in equal measure, and a rare amalgam of pastoral gifts. All we can say at this point is that the task of nurturing change is part and parcel of the faithful leader's role, and that if this vital role is missing, then good worship will prove elusive.

Now for the good news

Having reminded ourselves of some of the obstacles litter-
ing the path to creative and transformative worship, we
need to redress the balance. Fortunately our own efforts
are only half the story, for worship is a partnership with
God, a joint enterprise between human aspiration and the
infinite resources of 'the Lord, the giver of life'.[7]

The assembly of God's people gathered for worship is
drawn into a realization of its blessedness, into a discernment that not only is this holy ground, but that those
around them are holy people who have been charged with
the energy of God and irradiated with God's light. It is
here, at the gate of heaven, that we become fully ourselves, caught up by God's grace into a continual process
of transformation, changed 'from one degree of glory to
another'.[8]

Vital to this enterprise is the conviction that, by God's
grace, anything is possible for us. There is no reason
whatsoever why we, in our little tuppenny-ha'p'orth pile
of bricks, with all the limitations and handicaps we face,
cannot find worship inspiring and transforming, and our
weekly assembly a blurring of the boundaries of heaven
and earth. We need only big aspirations, an expectation
that, in Christ, the very best can be ours, and a willingness to work our socks off to make it happen.

Fundamental to the development of good worship is
the conviction that anything is possible, here in my small
corner, now in this present moment, as it was in the
Church of the Holy Wisdom, Constantinople, a millen-
nium ago. We need to live in the promise of God.

---

7 The Nicene Creed.

8 'And all of us, with unveiled faces, seeing the glory of the Lord as
though reflected in a mirror, are being transformed into the same image
from one degree of glory to another' (2 Corinthians 3.18).

Our part of the bargain is to make everything count; producing a memorable act of worship by making full and creative use of everything at our disposal. This simply means taking time whenever we gather for worship to consider carefully the setting, the number of participants, the occasion, the season, and the resources available, especially music. If attentive to every detail, we can tailor our liturgical suit according to the cloth available.

And there really is no excuse for not doing so. We have 2,000 years' experience behind us, we have a mountain of resources – textual, musical and technical – at our disposal, and now, thanks to the internet, we can drop in on other people's worship around the world, to taste and see.

When two people fall in love, they are inventing nothing new, and yet to them their love is like no other since time began. So it is with worship; we follow where countless others have trod, using a framework as old as the hills, and yet for us it will be new and exciting and special. To us, when we get it right, what we build together will seem unlike anything that has gone before. What we will discover, with this particular group of people, in this place and at this particular time, is unique.

All we are asked to do is to apply, with unfailing attentiveness, all our skills and our love to making whatever we do, and wherever we do it, an offering which in the words of Mother Teresa is simply 'something beautiful for God'.

PART 2

Building Blocks of Good Worship

Before we can begin to discern the chief characteristics of good worship, it is necessary to examine the circumstances in which it is most likely to flourish. Good worship doesn't just happen, but emerges from faith communities where certain prerequisites are already in place. These are the basic building blocks on which good worship is constructed.

I

Leadership

Every novelist needs an icicle in the heart.

Graham Greene[9]

Putting this section together involved several false starts because, no matter how hard one tries to focus on other possibly more exalted topics we might need to address at the outset, they all come back to leadership. Without good leadership, nothing very much is going to happen, and that needs to be faced at the start.

Of course I am beaten before I begin. There is no way of describing the kind of leadership required for good worship without someone out there getting the wrong end of the stick. So let it be said up front: no matter how big the heart or gentle the spirit of the true pastor, an inner core of single-mindedness verging on ruthlessness will also be required if ministry is to be truly Christlike. This applies particularly to worship.

Worship is a sphere of parish life where we all become conservatives, knowing what we like and defending it to the last. It takes a gifted leader to prise people away from adhesion to the familiar to the glimpsing of new possibilities; to mobilize a community to work towards the vision

---

9 Quoted in Ferdinand Mount, *Cold Cream: My Early Life and Other Mistakes*, 2009.

it has glimpsed; and to enter into new experiences of worship as a joyous adventure. Without strong, decisive leadership, good worship will remain a distant dream, an aspiration for another year, another generation.

The 'bible' of worship leadership is Robert Hovda's *Strong, Loving and Wise*[10] and the title says it all. In our current climate we are big on the loving bit, happy about the wisdom, but definitely get fidgety when it comes to exercising strength.

What we speak of here is true detachment; the ability to stand back from the emotive connection to discern dispassionately the way ahead. Doctors and social workers would collapse under the strain unless they learned detachment, and this applies equally to pastors.

'Strong leader' will inevitably be misread by some as 'control freak', but there is no intrinsic conflict between a clear and unwavering vision for what must take place, and a fully collaborative way of achieving it. It is perfectly possible to run a tight ship which is at the same time a happy ship, on which everyone feels they know where they are going and plays their part in getting there.

Those ordained to leadership in the church 'have meaning and reality only by virtue of their rootedness in the community',[11] and a good leader is as firm and decisive about ensuring that every member of the community feels included and empowered as she is firm and decisive about pushing ahead on the journey. Authentic, fruitful leadership emerges from the community, and is not set over against it.

In an age when interminable consultation is deemed necessary to change the proverbial light bulb, leadership

---

10 Robert Hovda, *Strong, Loving and Wise: Presiding in Liturgy*, 1976.

11 Cyrille Vogel, *Liturgy: Self Expression of the Church*, 1972, p. 19.

which is loving and gentle yet firm and decisive is pure gold.

Despite the best of intentions, some models of collaborative ministry inhibit boldness of action and exhaust the community with endless consultation before they ever reach the starting line.

Robert Warren once said of Vaclav Havel and Nelson Mandela that they showed themselves true prophets of our age by 'living by the values of the age to come'.[12] They had already entered, at least in part, the society to which they pointed in the darkest hours.

The true pastor today is no less a prophet, helping the community of faith, in times of frailty, disappointment, or mediocrity, to live the fullness and splendour of the future hope.

---

12 Canon Robert Warren, National Officer for Evangelism 1993–2004.

2

Building Community

So with yourselves; since you are eager for spiritual gifts, strive to excel in them for building up the church.[13]

The chief work of a good leader is to build community. The true pastor is one who works with devoted skill, tender loving care, and infinite patience to nurture a community of faith into fullness of being; surrendering to the work of the Spirit of God 'until all of us come to the unity of the faith and of the knowledge of the Son of God, to maturity, to the measure of the full stature of Christ'.[14]

Good worship springs from an authentic and palpable sense of community. Once we learn to 'cook on gas' as a genuinely interactive community of faith, we shall draw forth from one another a whole range of talents and ministries to create extraordinary worship. Although worship can and does happen at gatherings of strangers and on one-off special occasions, good worship at the local level, week in week out, depends very much on the quality of common life enjoyed by that local community. Good worship begins with a whole and happy community.

It cannot be done the other way round, for worship used as sticking plaster for a dysfunctional community

---

13 1 Corinthians 14.12.
14 Ephesians 4.13.

will not last very long. It is not much use devising creative acts of worship which we hope will somehow put the community back together again. The human heart is stubborn and contrary, and conflict will need to be addressed and wounds healed. We cannot look the other way when our community is hurting inside, for good worship will continue to be beyond us if we are not right with one another, not at ease with who we are as a body.

Building community is the first priority therefore of a church intent on renewing its worship. This demands a great deal of hard, intentional work, recognized as a corporate priority and involving several factors.

It is said of the writer Somerset Maugham[15] that as a young trainee doctor in a deprived area of London in the 1890s, 'confronted by such a variety of character and human type . . . he was enthralled by the narratives that day after day were spun out before him, excited by their indefinable potential'.[16]

Community building requires first a pastor who is above all excited by the indefinable potential of human beings, not apologizing for his curiosity but harnessing our similar natural inquisitiveness for the kingdom of God, longing to know what stories lie behind the faces, what makes people tick.

The pastor needs to be enthralled and fascinated not just by individuals but by the chemistry of their interaction, by the mechanisms which trigger a sense of community, binding together and energizing a mixed bag of individuals for the work of the kingdom of God.

Second, it requires a programme of community building that will embrace many aspects of our common life,

---

15 (William) Somerset Maugham, novelist and playwright 1874–1965.

16 Selina Hastings, *The Secret Lives of Somerset Maugham*, 2009.

providing various opportunities for members of the community to get to know one another better, to listen to one another and to strengthen the bonds which tie them together.

Coffee after worship, events which combine elements of worship, spiritual formation and socializing, small groups providing opportunities to learn, worship and shared meals in a home setting, pilgrimages, retreats, outings, and working groups to tackle particular projects, are all ways of building up a sense of belonging and common purpose.

The parish weekend has a particular role as an accelerant of community building. More can be achieved in one residential weekend away than in a whole year's programme back home. The effort involved first time round is considerable, but such is the nature of a well-run weekend that this year's nervous attendee is next year's recruiting sergeant. Huge strides forward in bringing a community to a sense of common purpose and eagerness for action can be achieved in 48 hours away from it all.

Undergirding all this will be a constant sensitivity, on the part of both pastor and people, to the health and well-being of the community of faith. Noticing signs of strain or tiredness, spotting the disruptive person, guarding lovingly all that has been established, but constantly evaluating areas in need of further work and nurture.

But this is not all about being nice, especially in the early stages when the shape and style of the community-to-be is being sketched in outline. Tough decisions will have to be made, and maybe some noses put out of joint, if a mature faith community is to emerge, and it is no good simply looking the other way and hoping for the best. When people threaten to leave, it will be sometimes appropriate to offer them the bus fare.

When gathered for worship we need to *look* like a community, not a collection of individuals barely on speaking terms, scattered across the room. We need to stop the clock, knock a few heads together and start again. The fellow curate in my training parish once refused to begin the Mass until the congregation, dispersed across the church, had moved to be in close proximity with him and with one another. There followed a few anxious moments before the reluctant regrouping began, but it worked because they knew he was not bluffing.

But the congregation aware of the need to build community, ready to enter into the enterprise with energy and enthusiasm, and willing to face the necessary change and upheaval, will experience a transformation which previously hardly seemed credible. They will emerge blinking into the sunlight of a new day, proclaiming, in the words of Dag Hammarskjold:

For all that has been, thanks
For all that shall be, yes![17]

---

17 Dag Hammarskjold, *Markings*, 1972.

3

Creating Assembly

The assembly of the baptized comes first, and the fundamental reality of ministry is the ministry of the entire
servant church.[18]

Creating assembly takes us a step further than building
community, for it moves us beyond a sense of social ease
and mutual respect and love to a profound awareness of
who we are under God and of the task set before us.

Growing awareness of our call to be God's holy assembly is a fundamental prerequisite of good worship. We
need to realize who we are and where we have come
from.

'Assembly' is a word which in the Judeo-Christian
tradition is central to our understanding of God's covenant people who, escaping from slavery in Egypt, began
a long journey into the promise of God. Through the
wilderness experience they were brought to a promised
land, but more important still, to an understanding of
God's covenant with them as his chosen people. Threaded
through the Hebrew Scriptures is the understanding of the
people of Israel as the holy assembly gathered by God –
the *qahal Yahweh* – the people of God called by Yahweh,
for whom 'God's holiness was communicated . . . in the

---

18 Hovda, *Strong, Loving and Wise*, p. 3.

assembly'.[19] Only in the assembly was self-realization of who they were called to be made possible.

As the first Christians slowly emerged from the structures of Judaism into a distinct and separate body of belief, it was natural that they would carry with them a strong sense of the holy assembly gathered by God. 'The apostolic church clearly understood itself as the continuation of Israel in general and of the qahal Yahweh in particular.'[20] Jesus himself, 'having this nomadic spiritual tradition in his bloodstream, embraced a peripatetic ministry',[21] and his followers continued to live out that journey, a people of the Way, more at home in tents than in temples.

Not surprisingly the infant Church developed rituals of its own appropriate to its understanding of assembly, and the Christian body soon came to understand itself as a *liturgical* assembly. It continued the Jewish custom of the reading of the Law and the Prophets (and later its own sacred texts), but did so in the context of the ritual meal emblematic of the Christian Way.

In so doing it reinterpreted the whole temple sacrificial system. Not only did Christ himself now replace both the priesthood and the animal sacrifices, but he was seen as the high priest,[22] not of a distinct priestly caste, but of the whole assembly of God's people who would together share a priestly role: 'But you are a chosen race, a royal priesthood, a holy nation, God's own people.'[23]

Had Peter been a Geordie fisherman from North Shields instead of Capernaum, familiar with the Tyneside plural

---

19 Catherine Vincie, *Celebrating Divine Mystery*, 2009, p. 24.

20 Vincie, *Celebrating Divine Mystery*, p. 25.

21 Richard Giles, *Re-Pitching the Tent*, 1997, p. 20.

22 Hebrews 4.14.

23 1 Peter 2.9.

'yous' ('yous are a royal priesthood'), centuries of confusion would have been avoided and the individualistic doctrine of the 'priesthood of all believers' might not have seen the light of day. For it is not as individuals that we are called to share the priestly life of Christ (a community of countless priests . . . heaven forbid!) but as a single *assembly*.

The assembly which now gathers for Sunday worship week by week exercises a priestly ministry of reconciliation, standing between God and humanity. With Christ, we lay ourselves upon the altar in response to Paul's appeal; 'present your bodies as a living sacrifice, holy and acceptable to God, which is your spiritual worship'.[24]

We may begin by simply 'going to church' – to observe, to enjoy the space, to sit in the back row – but wherever we encounter good worship we are moved on, into a deeper reality of God's presence. We find ourselves caught up in rather more than we bargained for. We wake up to a realization of being part of something mysterious and wondrous, not made with hands or crafted by a commission, a structure comprised of human beings yet beyond human imagining; totally in the here and now, yet with one foot already in heaven.

Like the children in *The Lion, the Witch and the Wardrobe*[25] we fumble and tumble our way through a tiny nondescript door we have never even noticed before, and step into a whole new glorious world. Except that our new world is not fantasy, but the reality of the holy priestly assembly of God's people; flesh and blood irradiated by the Spirit of God.

---

24 Romans 12.1.

25 C. S. Lewis, *The Lion, the Witch and the Wardrobe: The Chronicles of Narnia*.

4

Including Children

And all who heard him were amazed at his understanding and his answers.[26]

An assembly without children is a deficient, incomplete assembly, not only because children are a vital chunk of any cross-section of humanity, nor because they represent our future, but because they are identified in the Judeo-Christian tradition as the bearers of the mystery, who with acute directness are capable of piercing the pretences and defences of adulthood.

Our scriptural tradition is threaded through with an emphasis on the spiritual capacity of children. In Isaiah's vision of the just reign of the ideal king, it is 'a little child' who will lead the work of reconciliation,[27] and the psalmist exults in the fact that even the babbling of babies is a form of praise to God, a truth which Jesus lights upon when answering the religious authorities critical of the children who cheered him on at his entrance into Jerusalem. He taunts them with lack of knowledge of their own Scriptures as he quotes Psalm 8; 'out of the mouths of infants and nursing babies you have prepared praise for yourself'.[28]

---

26 Luke 2.47.

27 Isaiah 11.6.

28 Psalm 8.2; Matthew 21.16.

In the story of his conversing as a 12-year-old with the learned rabbis gathered in the temple,[29] Jesus himself models the insight that when it comes to spiritual matters, 'the child is father of the man'.[30] Later, Jesus in his ministry engages in a 'dramatic reversal of the child's traditional status in ancient societies as a silent non-participant'[31] when he indignantly silences those who would exclude children from his presence by declaring that 'it is to such as these that the kingdom of God belongs'.[32]

He goes on to hammer home the point by recognizing childlikeness as a key to the kingdom: 'Whoever does not receive the kingdom of God as a little child will never enter it.'

Contemporary writers such as Gerard Pottebaum[33] recall us to the fact that ritual-making and story-telling are expressions of our natural sense of mystery and wonder, and that in these areas it is the child who is 'the natural', the adult who is stiff and awkward and forgetful of the sense of awe which life and death should elicit from us. The work of Jerome Berryman, founder of Godly Play, is another strong influence in the same direction.

The issue of children and worship has been subject to extremes. A long period of excluding children from worship, or at least marginalizing them, has been followed by a tendency to create acts of worship in which the childish replaces the childlike. 'All age worship' is too often a euphemism for baby worship which not only insults the

---

29 Luke 2.41–52.

30 William Wordsworth, 'My heart leaps up'.

31 Robert Funk and Roy Hoover (eds), *The Five Gospels: What Did Jesus Really Say?*, 1993, p. 89.

32 Mark 10.14.

33 Gerard Pottebaum, Director of Treehaus Communications, Loveland, Ohio.

intelligence of adults present but demeans and patronizes the children themselves.

The formation of an authentic assembly requires the presence and acceptance (not merely the toleration) of children, as having a legitimate part to play in making our worship whole and complete. The challenge is to incorporate children in worship in such a way that they feel valued and engaged, while making proper provision for instruction which is tailored to their particular needs and age group.

Children in fact are a good test of whether our worship is on the right track. Worship needs to be good enough to engage and delight *all* the children of God whether 8 or 80 years. Boring worship is an affront to God, let alone a turn-off for the assembly.

While we can never categorize any age group with a single characteristic, nevertheless experience shows that children are as capable as their seniors of expressing awe and wonder, indeed probably more so, being untrammelled by the cynical ways of the world. We do children a disservice by suggesting that they cannot be still or silent in worship, for who has not seen a hush descend on a group of children fascinated by something new or mysterious or sensational?

So, with good teaching backed up by responsible parenting, hushed silence is as appropriate to children in worship as frantic activity. But we have to provide something for children to be awestruck by, and certainly the tired old patterns of worship maintained over many decades simply will not do. Kids come, and kids go, because there is nothing there to hold them.

Worship capable of captivating and holding on to children will be characterized by worship spaces of sensational beauty, powerful signs and symbols that can be touched and handled as well as seen, leadership which is excited by what we are doing, music expertly played on appropriate instruments that will have us humming its tunes (and pondering its theology) throughout the week, movement and drama and fun interspersed with moments of total silence and awe, the recognition of every member of the assembly, youngest to oldest, as being a minister of the offering, and the opportunity for every member to be fully engaged.

In this context, withdrawal classes are not seen as 'getting the children out of the way' but as a moment in the liturgy when age groups divide in order to experience the Scriptures in a way appropriate to their needs. This should be seen as one class among many, with adult groups undertaking their own instruction and reflection on the Scriptures at the same time. All will be taking part in the ministry of the Word, dividing after the penitential rite and coming back together for the sharing of the peace and the procession to the altar table.

The bottom line, however, is that worship (even for those Sundays when their teachers are on holiday) must be good enough from start to finish to hold children's attention and nurture their spiritual growth, just as it must hold and feed the rest of us. Worship that is good for children is worship that is good for the rest of us; we all need to be held spellbound by the things of God.

5

Turning to the Sun

If you, even you, had only recognized the things that
make for peace.[34]

The sunflower is a wondrous detail of God's creation, tall
and erect and flamboyant, aristocratic yet easily grown in
a back garden. Its most notable characteristic is its ability
to turn its face constantly towards the sun arching across
the sky.

The assembly of God's people at worship is likewise not
called to static immobility, waiting as it were for God's
light to come and seek it out, but to a constant turning
towards the light and energy of God, wherever it is to be
found. The assembly is called not simply to be, to exist,
but to turn with longing towards the face of God.

My soul thirsts for God, for the living God.
When shall I come and behold
The face of God?[35]

The assembly aware of its calling and purpose therefore
comes to worship longing for God, and already disposed
to receive all that God has to offer. The assembly thus
disposed towards the things of God exhibits certain

34 Luke 19.41.
35 Psalm 42.2.

characteristics in which the Spirit of God finds fertile soil. Godfried Danneels identifies the fundamental attitude of those seeking to worship as 'receptivity, readiness to listen, self-giving and self-relativizing'.[36]

Good worship is created among those who are ready, predisposed to enjoy and to participate, eager to learn more, ready to give of themselves, and who do not think of themselves as the centre of the universe. It is borne on wings of faith of those who are willing 'no longer to retain the initiative',[37] who dare let themselves fall into the arms of God.

It is an attitude, says Danneels, 'of orientation towards God, readiness to listen, obedience, grateful reception, wonder, adoration and praise . . . an attitude of prayer, of handing ourselves over to God and letting his will be done in us'. Such attitudes betoken a contemplative spirit, and are at odds with the instincts which govern many of our waking hours as we grapple with humankind's need to promote self, compete, and succeed whatever the cost to others.

In contrast, worship requires a reflective spirit, humble before God and gentle with one another. Our full active participation in the liturgy is not activity as the world knows it, but arises from the nurture of this contemplative dimension to our lives.

When I worked in West Yorkshire, the nicest and most significant thing ever said about our parish community was that 'these people know how to worship'. It was a community that came together intent on worshipping God. They came ready to embrace the silence as well as

---

36 Godfried Danneels, 'Liturgy Forty Years After the Second Vatican Council', 2003, p. 10.

37 Marshall, *Renewal in Worship*, p. 14.

the exultation, stillness as well as joyful interaction. They also came expecting to participate, to work their passage on the journey, and this meant more than sharing the tasks that make worship possible, but extended to the welcome of the newcomer and the pastoral care of one another.

Above all they were an assembly with an approach to worship that was utterly natural. They were at home with God, relaxed and confident in what they were doing, yet always in awe at the privilege of being who they were called to be. They approached worship as a shared enterprise. Gone for ever was any sense of worship as a performance put on by the few for the many. There was no 'they' up front; this was *our* show.

Assemblies such as these do not grow on trees. They take an enormous amount of hard work, attention to detail, straight talking, and huge love. Those who belong to them will be people who each week look forward with anticipation to the gathering of the community around God's table. They will dread the thought of missing it. For they can never quite get over the fact that they are who they are and where they are, engaged in this incredibly moving, demanding yet energizing thing called worship – the liturgy – the work of the holy people of God.

Above all they will constantly be aware of their blessedness under God, conscious of the fact that, to use one of the favourite phrases of Chiara Lubich,[38] God loves them immensely. When we encounter and inhabit a congregation that has evolved into a liturgical assembly in all fullness of meaning, then are made real for us those wondrous words from Luke's Gospel:

---

38 Chiara Lubich, 1920–2008, Founder of the Focolare Movement.

Blessed are the eyes that see what you see! For I tell you that many prophets and kings desired to see what you see and did not see it, and to hear what you hear, and did not hear it.[39]

---

39 Luke 10.23–24.

6

Making Space

He will show you a large room upstairs, furnished and
ready. Make preparations for us there.[40]

A good indicator of the seriousness with which the assembly approaches the business of reimagining worship has,
interestingly enough, nothing to do with the written, or
spoken, or sung content of the worship itself. It is the
way in which it sets about creating a room that will fit its
needs as exactly as possible.

It works as an indicator because, whereas human nature
has developed the survival strategy of ignoring what it
doesn't like in the realm of ideas, it has no such defence
mechanism when it comes to physical change under its
nose. 'Change' as an abstract notion does little to disturb the even tenor of life in the mainstream church. Once
it crosses into the physical realm of the environment in
which we gather, change becomes a threat.

'Change' as a practical step to improve the way in which
the assembly does worship can, no matter how small or
sensible, provoke unease, dissension or downright opposi-
tion. Passions run high, and faith communities can divide
or splinter over such issues.

---

40 Mark 14.15.

Once again, good leadership is essential, to steer the community through a process of change in which physical alterations flow from an overarching vision based on clear theological and liturgical principle. All will be of a piece.

In a mature community with good leadership and a clear sense of its being and purpose, it will be possible to assure all concerned that no physical alterations will be made which do not make sense or do not further the worship and work of the people of God, while at the same time ensuring that, once the direction is set and the vision owned, whatever physical alterations are found to be necessary will be followed through boldly and resolutely.

The theological basis of, and design criteria for, the reordering of worship space is dealt with fully elsewhere[41] with some practical tips in Part 4, A Worship Checklist, below. The essential thing is for the room to *work* as a place where the assembly can be truly itself. For this it needs a room tailored to present-day needs with good facilities for the associated tasks of welcome, nurture and socializing. Above all the room should work for the community, not the community for the room.

Historical accuracy or aesthetic quality are to be valued, but remain secondary considerations to the primary need for the assembly to be able to do the work of God today. The theological thought forms of previous centuries may inform our thinking, but should not be allowed to control our worship.

In changing our worship space we begin always with what we have, revealing and highlighting the best features, but rethinking and reimagining the room as a

---

41 Giles, *Re-Pitching the Tent*.

liturgical pavement on which will be enacted our journey into future encounters with the living God who beckons us ever onwards.

In so doing we shall automatically make our rooms for worship more user-friendly for those with disabilities. Existing buildings present all kinds of obstacles for the disabled: handrails at chancel steps, like fixed ropes up a mountainside; and altar tables situated in the far distance surrounded by a fence at which all are expected to kneel.

Level floors end-to-end should be the order of the day for all our worship rooms, uninterrupted by fences and rails, steps and obstacles. This benefits the whole assembly, not just the elderly or infirm. Here good theology and good manners speak as one.

Relighting our room can also have a powerful impact on our worship. Clearing the space and moving the furniture around may not be enough if we are still left with a room illuminated by light fittings appropriate to an aircraft hangar. Worship demands intimacy as well as splendour, different moods to fit different acts of worship or different sections of a single service. Let theatre be our guide, with its ability to take a bare stage and through lighting alone create a baking desert in one scene, and a rain-swept heath in the next.

Our task is to create rooms for worship that get us to the starting line. Rearranging the furniture will not of itself secure good worship, but it will create the space in which good worship can flourish. Conversely, worship spaces which inhibit our aspirations, cramp our style and restrict us to a museum mentality, are a self-indulgence we can no longer afford.

7

Going Counter-Cultural

> Stand firm, therefore, and do not submit to a yoke of slavery.[42]

The only time the Christian Church was seen to be clearly and unequivocally leavening the dough of humanity was during the first three centuries of its existence, before it was ensnared and made captive by the establishment in its various forms. In that period it presented the world with a different option for living life – a counter-culture at odds with the prevailing mores of the time. From that counter-cultural stance it took on the world and won. Even if it turned out to be a pyrrhic victory, it was an astonishing turnaround.

For us today there are two areas where good worship can be seen to go against the grain of contemporary society, both outside and within the Church. Of course any movement founded on faith will be counter-cultural in our post-Christian era, but over and above the question of faith, good worship subverts the prevailing norms in two particular ways: worship in society and worship in the Church, as the following sections.

---

42 Galatians 5.1.

Worship in society

In a culture which often seems to be hyperventilating, crowding every minute with continuous sound and frantic activity, good worship reasserts the natural rhythm of life, establishing a regular pulse, acting as the pacemaker of humanity's heart.

Worship at its best eschews both constant sound and restless activity. It nurtures the contemplative spirit and is not afraid of silence or stillness. It says to the world 'slow down'. Worship enables us to be at peace with God and with ourselves, so that we fear nothing.

Look around you on your journey to work and see how many people appear frightened of silence, of gaps between conversations on their mobile or tracks on their iPod, their thumbs itching to send the next text message.

Here, amid all this busyness, is where worship comes into its own as that which stills the storm of our lives, calming our restlessness so that we may know and listen to God.

In a culture where everything is reduced to bite-sized chunks, where a short attention span is taken as read, good worship takes people seriously as human beings of immeasurable potential. It doesn't talk down, but instead raises hopes and aspirations, affirming that all things are possible to those who love God, and delighting in that reversal of the world's order which was central to the teachings of Jesus of Nazareth.

As God's community gathered in worship we are reminded constantly that spiritual realities make nonsense of social standing or the acquisition of wealth, for, as Paul describes, we are those who appear 'as poor yet making many rich; as having nothing yet possessing everything'.[43]

---

43 2 Corinthians 6.10.

Good worship scandalizes society by its insistence on the central importance of an activity which has no apparent purpose, no measurable end product, no calculable net profit. Good worship requires that for once we stop talking about ourselves, our rights, needs and our ambitions, and instead listen. Good worship simply says 'Be still and know that I am God'[44] and for modern humanity that can be scary stuff.

Worship in the Church

Sad to say, good worship also runs counter to much of the Church's own culture. There is a deeply rooted assumption throughout organized Christianity that the Church's primary responsibility is the maintenance of an unchanging order, ensuring that what has always been ever more shall be so.

In this misconception of its role the Church is aided and abetted by those in society who value the Church for its contribution to our architectural and historical heritage alone, and who accordingly resist, sometimes fiercely, any change to the fabric of its buildings or the language and patterns of its worship. By definition they are anxious that the living stones of the Church do nothing to disturb the dead ones. For them the Church is the last bastion against change in a world rapidly changing in every other sphere.

The Church for its part is all too happy to conform to this role, training and ordaining new generations of clergy cast in a caretaker mould, expected to do no more than provide pastoral care for the existing membership, and to keep the show on the road, ruffling as few feathers

---

44 Psalm 46.10.

as possible along the way. Continuing as before, perpetu-
ating the established pattern, has therefore become the
Church's default position.

Good worship can come as something of a shock in
this culture, for it bears the stamp of a Teacher who
destabilized the religious world of his day in order that
God might break through. Jesus in his teaching and ministry inverted almost every tenet of his own religious
tradition in order to reveal their true meaning and power,
and the Church in its primitive essence bore a presump-
tion for change. Only since it found itself in the year 312
unable to resist the lure of an emperor who came bearing
gifts has it become synonymous with stability, order and
resistance to change.[45]

Worship which is irradiated with the vitality of the
essential message of Jesus and his immediate followers
will, by its inevitable embrace of change as a primary
characteristic of the good news, appear to many in the
Church as uncomfortable, even threatening.

This is why any attempt to renew worship in the spirit
of the dynamic first centuries of the Church's existence
will inevitably involve a counter-cultural thrust that will
disturb the cosy little modus vivendi developed by mainstream Christianity over the centuries.

Such renewal will demand not merely learning a new
tune, but adopting a whole new song sheet. It will challenge the deep-seated resistance to change found almost
everywhere within the Church, and require a willingness
to reset the Church default position to its original pre-
sumption for change. This too is scary stuff.

---

45 In 312 Emperor Constantine was reputedly converted to Christianity
and thereafter played a leading role in the Church's further development
as an agent of stability throughout the Empire.

Renewing worship will therefore involve counter-cultural thrusts at odds with the current climate in both church and society. But in this work of God we shall be striving to create a new climate of opinion, a new way of working with one another, a new milieu in the local church spilling out into the world around us. In this new culture, change will once again be the regular currency in the life of God's people.

PART 3

Characteristics of Good Worship

Given that these building blocks, or at least some of them, are securely in place, what characteristics might then be discerned as marking good worship? What will 'good worship' look like, how will it feel?

We are talking here mainly about degree, rather than presence or absence. The components discussed below will be present in most acts of worship to some degree; there is nothing new here, no 'lost component' rediscovered. Rather we are talking about awareness and focus.

First an acute awareness on the part of the assembly of the presence of God in all things, of their call to be the people of God, and of the limitless potential of a life lived in God. Second, arising from a passionate conviction that worship is the key to all of life, a single-minded focus on the task of making worship as beautiful and as powerful as it can be.

Given these attitudes of heart and mind worship can become an experience which engages, inspires and transforms and which takes us to stand, at least for a moment, at the very gate of heaven.

8

Expectancy

The essence of the New Testament is being set free to worship properly.[46]

At the heart of good worship is the conviction that, right here, in this room, at this hour, anything could happen; a realization that worship takes place on the threshold of the realm of God, on the border between earth and heaven.

'The Spirit is with us'; we are not completely in charge. Although we plan and prepare, there remains a sense in which worship, by definition, must always remain beyond our control. A frisson of excitement and uncertainty runs through us as we prepare for this encounter. Conversely, if we don't expect that anything will happen, then probably nothing will.

We all know what Christmas Eve feels like. No matter for how many months we have been hearing carols in the shopping centre, no matter how often previous Christmases have left an empty feeling, we never quite lose our sense of childlike anticipation on this magic night. Even the hardened cynic wants it to snow.

Our gathering for Sunday worship is also a time of anticipation and promise, no matter how many times we

46 Rowan Williams, Annual Conference of the Council for the Care of Churches, Oxford, 2006.

have trodden this path before. We wait for the irruption of God's presence into the humdrum routine of our lives, never quite sure what might happen. We wake to this new morning with wonder, a little apprehensively, certainly with a quickening pulse, as we make our way to the place of meeting, reunion and celebration. If every Sunday is a mini-Easter, every Saturday night is a mini Christmas Eve.

The story is told of Michelangelo receiving into his workshop a large new slab of marble ready to be worked on. When asked what kind of figure he intended to make from it, he replied: 'I don't know, but I'll find out.' In other words he would approach with reverence the raw material given him and discover what lay within before discerning the figure that would finally emerge.

No more can we fully know what our Sunday worship will bring until we are actually doing it, chiselling away at the raw material God gives us; time, place, Scriptures, bread, wine and oil, and most wondrous of all, the human beings, with their gifts and aspirations, joys and trials, who will gather alongside us.

We gather together with reverence for this assembly of which we are part, and at a deeper level we submit ourselves to the presence of God with whom in this act we make rendezvous, the unknowable made known, yet always beyond us, unpredictable, unbiddable, untamed.

Paul warned the Christians at Corinth not to partake of the eucharistic meal 'without discerning the body',[47] for we must look beyond the surface appearance of things to recognize the reality before us, if only we have eyes to see. In worship we come into the presence of the Life-Giver, the source of all existence, the 'I AM'.

---

47 1 Corinthians 11.29.

At meetings or gatherings in all walks of life, there comes a moment just before things are about to begin, when silence falls, the murmur of voices ebbs away, and the audience, the participants, compose themselves; ready, focused, expectant. Sometimes this happens naturally, at other times (in fact most of the time), we have to give a helping hand.

Waiting for worship to begin I have recently been treated to a discussion on comparative quotes for gutter replacement, and to hearing lengthy detailed navigational directions shouted into a mobile phone by a man pacing up and down the aisle. Such bad habits are all too common an indicator of a failure to recognize the nature of the event in which we are about to take part, an inability to discern not just that this is holy ground, but that those around us are holy people.

How might we help create a culture of expectancy in which silence falls naturally?

Silence

At the Theatre Royal, Newcastle, a few minutes before a performance is to begin, the auditorium is filled for a moment with the amplified sound of mobile phones ringing. No words are needed; the audience gets the message and after a flurry of searching in pockets and bags, stillness descends.

Silence is the chief ingredient of a corporate sense of expectancy. When something big is about to happen, we shut up. Silence is a sure sign that we mean business, we are ready to go. Even the rustling of a sweet wrapper is regarded as letting the side down.

Layout

Wherever possible the ministry of welcome should be separated out from the worship room. Welcome should be a warm and unrestrained affair, unfettered by taking place in the same space where people are trying to prepare quietly for worship.

Where such separation of uses is not physically possible, those greeting participants at the door should be trained to convey, by their own demeanour, their own sense of suppressed excitement, the fact that worship is about to begin and that everyone is invited to join the others in quiet preparation.

Preparation

The room should be still, with minimal dashing about by those making preparations, and a mood of recollection created by appropriate music. Where skilled musicians are not available, recorded music will serve very well. Once the mood is established, silence can precede the actual beginning of worship.

Another means of establishing a sense of expectancy is to provide an opportunity, for those who wish it, to sing (or say) together a simple version of Morning Prayer about 30 minutes before the main act of worship is due to begin. This establishes an air of expectancy and prayerfulness which is fairly easy to maintain through the intervening period when others will be entering the room.

Teaching

Once worship begins, the assembly will take its cue from those leading worship. From the very first announcement or greeting, those addressing the community need to convey their own sense of expectancy, excitement and delight in what they are doing.

No opportunity should be lost by the leaders of worship to remind, explain and exhort the assembly to remember what its gathering is all about. This needs just a light touch on the tiller – an introductory or link sentence here or there – but provides a constant corrective to the course to be navigated, recalling us to the shared vision, instilling a sense of wonder, and gently but firmly ensuring that nothing is allowed to devalue or derail the act of worship.

Posture

All members of the assembly play their part, chiefly by their own demeanour and posture. Posture is an area of which we need to be more aware in enhancing an attitude of expectancy. Body language speaks volumes.

A deep bow on entering the room; bows exchanged between president and people at the beginning of worship; sitting upright with hands open and extended in preparation; standing to pray together, with heads erect and hands open and lifted in the *orans* posture of the early Church; all these signs of attentiveness, readiness and humble receptiveness will help heighten a sense of expectancy.

Poor posture is a telltale sign of an assembly unaware of its role and of a leadership that has abdicated its responsibility for liturgical formation. The prime example is the phantom kneel. Congregations which claim they kneel to pray largely delude themselves. What happens in reality is that people crouch forward in their seats, forehead held in one hand, in a posture which suggests despair and indifference in equal measure. The hassock hangs unused on its hook or gathers dust on the floor.

From earliest times the assembly stood to pray (indeed kneeling was deemed inappropriate on Sunday, the day of celebration).[48] When we pray as a body therefore, we need to emerge from the cramped and confined postures of the recent past, and instead stand upright, with heads held high, and with confidence claim the promises, as befits the sons and daughters of God.

Neighbours from other faith traditions, especially Sikhs and Muslims, recall us to another ancient tradition of removing our shoes on entering the place of worship, a custom originating in the Judeo-Christian tradition with Moses who, before the burning bush, was told 'Come no closer! Remove the sandals from your feet, for the place on which you stand is holy ground.'[49]

It is a thousand pities that somewhere along the line we dropped the ball on that one. Removing one's shoes leaves us feeling, in some visceral way, exposed and vulnerable, which is no bad thing when approaching heaven's gate. We would have grown less careless of the mystery had we maintained this ancient practice, and scrabbling around in the church porch amid a mountain of shoes every Sunday after worship might have rubbed a few edges off us in the Body of Christ.

48 'The early church never lost this conception of Sunday as . . . a day of praise and triumph. Fasting and the penitential observance of kneeling in prayer were strictly forbidden.' R. F. Buxton, *A New Dictionary of Liturgy and Worship*, 1986, p. 500.

49 Exodus 3.5.

9

Presiding

The beauty and nobility of this office, or function, or service is so great that the church's call to its exercise should be an overwhelming experience for anyone, veteran or novice.[50]

Presiding at worship is the supreme privilege of those who exercise leadership in the church, and how well they rise to the occasion will be one of the biggest single factors in determining the character of the worship. The effective president is not only a good teacher, but a good model. Although we may all have our own model of presidency based perhaps on a pastor who played a part in our formation, nevertheless it is possible to discern some common denominators of good presidency.

Humble

While exercising confidently the gifts and skills necessary to the task, the president will be at the same time overwhelmed by the enormity of what she is asked to be and to do. When we lose the butterflies in the stomach before we approach this task, it is time to hang up the alb for the last time.

---

50 Hovda, *Strong, Loving and Wise*, p. 18.

From the president's own sense of awe and wonder at her calling will the entire assembly catch the bug, and develop its own sense of wondrous reverence.

Competence

Some clergy contrive to lead worship as if they have just woken from a long sleep that morning to find themselves ordained. They act as if they have never been in church before, let alone led worship, as they emerge from the dark, blinking at the sunlight. Good worship demands a high degree of competence, and amateurishness in leading worship is not a sign of humility but of hubris, suggestive of casualness and having nothing to learn. The person who presides needs to be on top of the job, clued up, acutely aware, and simply good at it.

Choreographer

The president is above all the choreographer of the great joyous dance of the people of God in worship.

On occasions this will involve a literal dance – if the conclusion of the Easter Vigil, for example, does not get the whole assembly up on its feet dancing then something is seriously amiss – when the president with two left feet will be thankful to have been spared ordination in the Coptic Church, where the ability to dance is a prerequisite of holy orders.

But at every Sunday gathering for worship a dance is taking place, albeit a figurative one, in that the offering of a dynamic community of love and praise is a dance of the heart in the presence of God. The role of the president is to get everyone up on their feet – often before they realize it – to produce an act of worship to God which is stunning in its joy and praise, its dynamism and movement. There should be no wallflowers feeling excluded in this dance hall.

John Betjeman was once described as another Diaghilev, enchanting all he came into contact with and 'making them feel that theirs is the only universe that counts, and that they are kings of it'.[51]

Like a good dancing master, the president knows his 'dancers', his 'cast', that is, all who come ready to worship and to participate fully, and has a gift for enabling everyone to feel good about themselves, noticed and listened to, and to achieve things they previously thought beyond them. He helps them to feel like 'kings' in whatever task is assigned to them.

In so doing, the president earns, through dedication, hard work and good humour, the respect and affection of those she leads.

In charge

The president is the person in charge of the worship, the one who holds it all together. Through his gifts it has shape, and pace and direction.

A good president will be *in charge,* but will never dominate. At the scene of a road accident we don't need a well-meaning passer-by but a highly trained paramedic; here is someone who *knows what they are doing*, and will tell us what to do, so that we may be truly useful rather than getting in the way.

If the president is unsure and hesitant, forever scrabbling about for the right bit of paper, if her first words

---

51 Ferdinand Mount, *Cold Cream*, p. 66.

to the assembly are 'is this working?', as she frantically taps the microphone, then we know we are in trouble. The liturgy needs to take off crisply, boldly and with an air of authority. We can then relax into the journey of worship.

The first sign of proficiency will be worship that begins bang on time. There is no excuse for a late start, neither the failure of key players to show up, nor the particular culture of a congregation. The good president knows how to improvise as occasion demands, even to preach at a moment's notice. No matter what crises hit the sacristy, the show must go on, and go on as if nothing whatsoever is amiss.

The president will at times be required to maintain law and order, intervening decisively, even sharply, when someone's lack of awareness disrupts worship for others (chatting at the altar while awaiting communion is a recently observed example), or when the best-laid plans go awry and a split-second judgement call is needed.

Narrator

The president's voice is that which begins and ends worship and which is threaded through the whole action, providing unity and cohesion. His voice frames every section, no matter how many different voices are heard, or how much delegation occurs.

In eucharistic worship, the president always greets the assembly, says the prayer of the day, pronounces the absolution, invites the assembly to affirm their faith, to offer prayers, and to share the peace, leads the eucharistic prayer, and pronounces the blessing if there is one. Hers is the first and last voice heard (unless there is a deacon or other liturgical minister present to give the dismissal).

Good worship is not a series of unconnected variety acts following on one from another, but a single cohesive whole in which there are several parts and many voices. The president embodies this cohesion by being there throughout and by introducing and concluding each component. No matter how much is delegated to others, the president remains the delegator and the one to whom the direction of proceedings is returned after others have played their part.

Narration is a skilful art because, essential though it is, it should be done with such a sure and light touch that we hardly notice it. Recently at Sunday worship I was treated to the announcement of every single hymn even though the numbers were both on a board and in the service leaflet. We were also told that the service began on page 1.

Model

The president embodies the aspirations of the whole assembly. It is the leader, in his bearing and manner, in his excitement at the possibilities, his composure and quiet assurance, who will instil in the whole assembly the qualities that will make its worship striking, memorable, and transformative.

The assembly will 'catch' from the good leader the virus of attentiveness, of knowing oneself to be in the presence of God. The assembly will learn from the president the attitudes appropriate to the occasion, and will take their cue from him. A competent president can calm people's restlessness (even get them to stop leafing anxiously through their orders of service for a lost page), helping them take from her a sense of resting calmly in the presence of God.

Conversely, a leader who is agitated and distracted in the lead-up to worship will infect all those leading alongside him, and the whole congregation, with his busyness and lack of inner peace.

Slapdash worship starts and finishes with the president: if his posture spells a casual amateurish approach – sitting cross-legged, hands forever fiddling and moving around – this soon spreads throughout the assembly. The president carries the burden of embodying the worship of the whole group, and his body language must be measured and impeccable.

It may suit the lazy president to imagine that such details do not matter, but unfortunately they do. The sacramental power of small things to give big messages works in both negative and positive directions.

Invisible

Strange as it may seem, the good president is able to take centre stage yet remain almost unseen; he is everywhere and nowhere, fully in charge but practically invisible. This is possible in so far as the president, while fully aware of his authority, is so at peace with himself and his role that the part he plays will never appear assertive or intrusive.

The president is therefore very far from being a control freak, but someone who exercises leadership by being in command but *without anyone realizing it*, so seamlessly will the liturgy flow, so naturally will one person take over from another in facilitating the various segments of the rite.

In a popular episode of *Keeping Up Appearances,* Mrs Bouquet was able to mistake the earl for the gardener, when visiting a stately home, because he was genuine top drawer, not someone (like Mrs B herself) striving to put on airs and graces, attempting to be someone he was not.

The good president is likewise someone relaxed about authority while nevertheless exercising it, not feeling it necessary to put on airs or dominate the proceedings, but delighting in seeing others blossom and grow. In this way the assembly becomes comfortable with itself also, its members happy to be who they are, delighting in what they are called to be and to do.

In relationship

A good president has a clear sense of her being first and foremost *part of the assembly*, rather than a dignitary set over it. This enables her to deal easily and effectively with the hundred little things that go towards making good worship. Because she has first established the basic relationships of loving mutual support which is the mark of a mutual assembly, everything else becomes possible. The heights can be scaled because base camp is well located, organized and provisioned.

While this is true of leadership for worship in general, it is supremely true of the president of the Eucharist. The president's role here is of crucial importance if the worship of the assembly of God's people is ever to take off rather than amble down the runway flapping its wings hopefully.

The language we use to describe this process may vary – we may refer to this as 'every member ministry', or the 'full, conscious and active participation'[52] of all the faithful – but it all boils down to the same thing: the

---

52 Second Vatican Council, The Constitution on the Sacred Liturgy II.14.

process whereby in worship we are changed from specta-
tors into participants, receivers into givers.

For the president presiding with a sense of being *en
famille*, among her own, even the mistakes will be turned
into moments when the assembly relaxes and laughs
together, or a member is encouraged and reassured, or an
omission is made good in a creative and helpful way.

Sometimes there will be bad habits to correct and
inconsiderateness to others to be nipped in the bud.
Like a good community police officer widely known and
respected, the president who is in relationship with her
people will be able to deal with problems in the assembly
with a light touch and a dose of humour before they get
out of hand.

Presence

Above all the good president will have developed a *presence*, that indefinable and elusive yet essential gift of the
born teacher who does not have to shout, but whose
students hang on his every word. This is evident the
moment the opening greeting of the liturgy (no, not 'good
morning') is announced with great strength, confidence
and aplomb but without theatricality. If these first few
seconds go well, the rest follows; we are in for something
memorable and good. Instead of watching the clock, we
will not want it to end.

Even before a word is spoken, the leader's sense of
presence can communicate itself to the whole assembly.
The hubbub fades away, and silence falls, and all present
are enabled to give themselves with acute attentiveness
to the work of the people of God. A leader with presence knows what is appropriate and when, and has (for
aren't all clergy alleged to be frustrated actors?) a highly

developed sense of timing, and of the acute particularity of 'the moment'.

Signpost

John the Baptizer famously said of Jesus that 'he must increase, but I must decrease',[53] and the good president, even as she holds the reins firmly in her hands, seeks always to slip away quietly from prominence in order that the assembly may come into its own, and God be glorified. The president *points away from self* so that the liturgy is never intruded upon by personality or appearance, habits or mannerisms, likes or dislikes.

As Robert Hovda reminds us, the liturgy, for all its apparent powerlessness, 'keeps alive a kingdom vision', and for the president 'to preside in the very deed that so expands the life of creatures is a function of unquestionable beauty and nobility'.[54] It doesn't get much better than that.

53 John 3.30.
54 Hovda, *Strong, Loving and Wise*, p. 19.

10

Engagement

Religion isn't where your mind is. Religion is where your ass is.[55]

Good worship is engaged with the world which gives it context. It is rooted in the soil of the local cultural landscape, and occurs in a moment of actual time. Because good worship seeks not only to give glory to God but also salt, and light, and flavour to the world, it needs to be firmly rooted in the ground on which it is set. Good worship holds together in one event both a stepping back from, and at the same time a connecting with, all that is going on around us.

Engagement operates at several levels:

With the local community

The emergency services' sirens piercing the quietest moments of our worship are no bad thing (and even the bullet holes in the external walls of Philadelphia Cathedral after one Saturday night shoot-out had a part to play). They remind us that, when we gather to do the work of the people of God, we straddle the divide between physical

---

55 Philip Berrigan, priest and anti-war activist, 1923–2002.

and spiritual realities, and between all that is beauteous and beastly in humankind.

Our engagement is a two-way street. The local church in some way sanctifies the community, the place, in which it is set, but the local community, with its own character and grit and edge, gives to the church in its midst that priceless gift of time and place, which is our Nazareth.

Nothing could be sadder than the phenomenon of the ghetto church, clinging fiercely to its past, supported only by those who long ago moved away to the suburbs, and as connected to its neighbourhood as a space landing craft resting on the surface of the moon. Its worship may be perfectly 'correct', but if it is irrelevant to all who live in its neighbourhood, it died long ago.

It does not take much to make a connection. A church near here on the Northumberland tourist trail is always open, sparkles with good care, has a good display of the recent events and smiling faces, and makes a real attempt to connect with the passer-by. Near the doorway is placed a deep jar of water alongside which is a cup full of small pebbles. A card explains that this is their 'prayer pool', and invites the visitor to place a pebble in the water 'for someone you want to immerse in God's all surrounding love'.

That's engagement.

With other churches

Mainstream churches find it hard to accept lessons from other ecclesial communities such as the community churches, now a feature of many major towns, whose premises often boast every conceivable modern facility and auditoria seating thousands.

They need lots of seats because they have learned to

speak the language of contemporary culture, in its building, its outreach and above all its worship. Everything is translated into the experience of contemporary society; it is connected, engaged, and people flock to it.

By contrast we appear like an Edwardian family gathered round a pianola on a Sunday evening, we just turn the handle of the worship machine and the same old stuff comes tumbling out – 'look, no hands!' we cry delightedly.

With the arts world

The world of theatre is able, with a handful of actors and a modicum of lighting equipment, to create not just different moods, but to transport us to any place in the world at any time in history.

In the Royal Shakespeare Company's 2009 production of *Julius Caesar*, superb acting was matched by brilliant technical expertise. By projecting onto a series of revolving panels moving images of soldiers locked in hand-to-hand fighting, the relatively small cast of 15 or so actors was enabled to bring to life the noise and commotion of a battlefield of thousands.

Imagine such creativity transposed to the drama of a Eucharist in a cathedral or large parish church; images of the 'angels and archangels and the whole company of heaven' suddenly appearing around the altar at the *sanctus*, or of areas of the world ravaged by warfare or famine at the prayers of the people. But we are left standing.

In 1996 Bill Viola's video image *The Messenger*[56] was projected onto the west end of Durham Cathedral; a powerful and captivating image which drew thousands

---

56 Bill Viola, artist and pioneer of architectural video installations.

to come and gaze. Significantly, however, this installation was seen as part of 'the arts', quite separate from 'worship'. The two categories inhabited watertight compartments. We may use artists to decorate our house but rarely invite them to eat at our table.

With the world

The conflicts that now consume our world, fanned by the fundamentalism and fanaticism which seem to be increasing their hold on all major faith traditions, indicate that humanity learns nothing from the lessons of history and continues its brutal way. This is the background against which our worship takes place.

Appalling though the agony of the world is, it sharpens the challenge to men and women of faith to put into practice the teachings of Jesus, to love our enemies and those who persecute us, to renounce suspicion and mistrust, and to reject any form of extremism that puts religious dogma before God. These healing insights should be evident in our worship, even on those Sundays when the sun shines and the birds sing.

With the wider Church

Our worship needs to be shown to be part of a worldwide movement of praise and thanksgiving to God, of which we are but a small part; we are not in liturgical solitary confinement. We do not choose readings to suit ourselves, but use those given to keep us connected to the rest of the worldwide Church; we say the prayer of the day to keep us connected to the Church's year; we pray for our bishop or regional leader, to remind us of the larger unit of which we are an integral part and of those who have the 'care of all the churches'.[57]

With other faith traditions

Post 9/11 we have woken up in an increasingly polarized world which makes engagement with other faiths more urgent and important than ever. One of my most treasured liturgical possessions is a long white silk scarf given to me by the Tibetan Buddhist teacher Lohsang Santem, after he and I had worked together on a shared prayer project in Philadelphia.

Lohsang spent two weeks with us in the cathedral building a *mandala*, a prayer made of countless grains of coloured sand. Because it is a living tradition, he included not only the Buddha, but Jesus alongside him. But as significant as the painstaking building was the ritual destruction at the end, and the procession to the river to throw the sand back into the sea. He taught us much about creation and the transitory nature of all things, even those which we craft and treasure. Crowds came to watch enthralled.

Within worship

Engagement is equally important *within* the faith community gathered for worship. From the moment we enter the worship space a sense of engagement between us and between regulars and visitors should be self-evident. Does the person who greets you at the door (if anyone does) *engage* with you, or do you get only a sideways glance as he continues to chat to a friend?

57 2 Corinthians 11.28.

As worship begins does the leader of worship *engage* with the assembly, directly and naturally, in a personal, warm, and direct way, or does he appear distant, distracted, or even bored? As the worship continues is the newcomer made to feel part of the enterprise or something of an interloper in others' domesticity?

The members of the assembly must also play their part. Does it behave like a mature community, open, friendly and at ease with itself yet inclusive of others? Watch for the sharing of the Peace: if the regulars indulge in a love-in while the newcomer is left standing, then you will recognize a church that is 'friendly', but only with its own.

An engaged assembly is above all one where each participant will feel themselves *known*. On Easter Day in a local parish this year, a joyous and exciting act of worship culminated in the parish priest's throwing crème-eggs into the congregation for people to catch, and as he did so he was able to call out their names. He was a priest engaged with his congregation; they were a people who were known and valued.

The greater the sense of engagement, the more each member of the assembly will feel their interconnectedness with others at every level and in every sphere. Holding hands to say the Lord's Prayer, they will know that the circle is not confined to that room, but spans barriers of culture, class and creed.

11

Timelessness

I know a person in Christ who fourteen years ago was caught up to the third heaven – whether in the body or out of the body I do not know; God knows. And I know that such a person – whether in the body or out of the body I do not know; God knows – was caught up into Paradise and heard things that are not to be told, that no mortal is permitted to repeat.[58]

Engagement is, however, only half the story; engraved on the obverse side of the coin of worship is transcendence, or timelessness. The paradox of good worship is that while it bids us step fully into time and place, at the same time it lifts us out of time, and more deeply into the mystery.

'When we drink a cup of tea very deeply,' wrote Thich Nhat Hanh, 'we touch the whole of time.'[59] When in worship we penetrate beyond the appearance of things and actions to their deepest meaning and significance, we relegate time to a notion of secondary importance. The significance of *being* wells up within us to quieten the urgency of *doing*.

To enter into an awareness of timelessness therefore is not about a striving to experience something beyond us,

---

58 2 Corinthians 12.2–4.
59 Thich Nhat Hanh, *Living Buddha, Living Christ*.

but rather a surrendering, a letting go, in order to enter fully and unconditionally into everything we do. The most mundane ordinary act, by its very simplicity and purity, can purvey a sense of the eternal realities. If this is true of drinking a cup of tea, so much more deeply and wondrously is it true of offering worship.

When, through our letting go to enter more deeply, we nurture this sense of timelessness, we begin to perceive the true meaning of things and to acquire the wisdom that comes from God alone. When we open and unfold the sacred Scriptures set in the midst of the assembly, and hear not simply a series of words but the timeless cry and longing of the people of God and God's response of grace and love, we begin to see its meaning. When we as an assembly share a loaf and a cup of wine, we see not just a ritual act but a participation in the timeless offering of he who gave this sign in an upper room, on the road and by the shore.

It is ironic that a frequent first response to the renewal of worship or the redesign of worship space is one of fear that we shall 'lose transcendence'. As if our tired, pedestrian, antique worship patterns were transcendent, timeless and full of mystery!

We urgently need to create good worship capable of transporting us from the hackneyed and mundane into a different world, in which time seems suspended, and we immerse ourselves in the mystery which is Emmanuel, God with us. The Orthodox tradition corrects at one stroke our Western busyness by declaring the Eucharist to be 'the Holy Mysteries' of God, celebrated in a building which is 'the earthly heaven in which the heavenly God lives and moves'.[60]

---

60 Ware, *The Orthodox Church*, p. 269.

As well as completely engaging us, body, mind and soul, in the here and now, good worship rescues us from the tyranny of the pressing moment. It remains unfathomable, impenetrable, quite beyond us. Like walkers on the high hills entering the cloud layer, in worship we are enveloped in our own 'cloud of unknowing'[61] that we may eventually come to know all things. Being brought into a deeper love for God we are given the joyous recognition of ourselves as the beloved of God, sought out, named, forgiven and healed. 'Now I know only in part; then I will know fully, even as I have been fully known.'[62] It is in this wondrous knowledge, still not fully grasped or understood, that we stand at the very gate of heaven.

Even in our hyperactive culture it is perfectly possible to breathe a proper sense of timelessness into any act of worship, but we shall need to be intentional about it. As in so many aspects of worship, the president has the key role. She can slow the pace, calm the atmosphere, banish anxiety and outlaw haste. In her own person, by her bearing and body language, the president can embody a sense of timelessness in our Sunday worship.

The Eucharist in particular is a form of worship in which a sense of timelessness is most readily engendered. Because at its heart is a simple ritual act common to all humanity in all places and in all ages, we are lifted, if we allow ourselves to be, out of the immediate into the eternal.

As we give thanks to God over bread and wine, we can be transported, once we allow our imagination to take wings, to a little house on the side of a dusty track en route to Emmaus, to a catacomb beneath first-century

---

61 The title of an anonymous work of Christian mysticism, written in Middle English in the early fourteenth century.
62 1 Corinthians 13.12.

Rome, to a wattle and daub hut at the time of Alban, or a small monastery on the Northumberland coast in the eighth century as the Danish boats menaced on the horizon. Like a telescope being rammed shut, time will collapse as we ponder the eternal and unchanging significance of the mystery in which we are engaged.

The lesson for us is to be less immediate, less pushy with God, less frantic about the things we have to fit into our day, which press in upon us at worship and rob us of peace. As my daughter would say, we need to chill.

12

Silence

There is nothing so much like God as silence.[63]

Silence is the one precious thing, free of charge, that every act of worship can give us. It is available to all, anywhere, anytime, and is the biggest single ingredient of that sense of timelessness we have just spoken of.

The absence of intentional silence in regular Sunday worship is inexplicable and inexcusable. Leaders of worship are offered silence on a plate – it requires no permission from on high, no resolution of the church council – and yet still spurn its use, evidently unaware of its potential impact or nervous about how to introduce or manage it.

Silence belongs to everyone, a treasure waiting to be found. We just have to uncover it and let it speak. Silence is made even more desirable by our daily exposure to noise as the wallpaper of our daily existence. Noise is now the inescapable background to anything we do in the public realm. That's our world.

For this reason worship should come into its own as one of the few places in the contemporary world where humanity can be reacquainted with silence. To be still, to be acutely aware of one's surroundings, to bask in silence,

---

63 Meister Eckhart 1260–1328.

is to find an oasis of cool water and luxuriant green after a long desert journey. It seems almost a mirage, too good to be true, but worship can do it, if we allow it to.

Silence is invaluable in good worship as a means of stilling our frantic spirits, of sifting through our thoughts and concerns to enable God alone to rise to the surface to be, for a few moments at least, the focus of our being, that 'our hearts may surely there be fixed where true joys are to be found'.[64]

So if worship is going to be worship in all its fullness it will need to include periods of silence to help us step aside, at least for a few moments, from the headlong rush of the lemmings, and allow God to speak to our hearts. Silence will offer us a chance to glimpse a deeper reality, to see things as they really are, and help us cultivate a deep interior peace. It will enable us to embrace stillness, gratefully and joyfully.

Unlike acts of worship which may consist entirely of silence (as that of the Society of Friends for example), we are talking here of a creative interplay between words, song, action and silence, each playing their part, each sharpening our appreciation of the other. G. K. Chesterton's dictum that 'there is a moment when the road points to the pub, and a time when the pub points to the road', applies well to worship. When we have been busy singing and doing for a while, we long to sit and be still. Refreshed by a time of silence, we long to be moving again.

Pascal once said that all our troubles come from our inability to be alone in a dark room. We are nervous of silence, on our own, in worship, because we are not sure what it will bring to light. Our worship tends to be full of unceasing sound, and constant activity. Products of our

---

64 *Common Worship 2000*, Collect for the Third Sunday before Lent.

time, we see silence as an intrusion, an unproductive lull in the proceedings, frustrating our need to move on. We find ourselves embarrassed by silence, not sure what to do with it.

Peter, James and John on the Mount of Transfiguration felt the need to jabber away about practical things because the glory was too much for them. Peter 'did not know what to say, for they were terrified'.[65] Likewise we pack our worship time with music and speech and language or the showing of visual imagery, to avoid those 'awkward silences' when we fear we will not know what to do in our conversation with God. We rarely shut up.

Silence in worship is difficult simply because we have not been taught to use it. If we are to relax into silence, and appreciate it as an end in itself, not just as a transition between other sections of our worship, it will require proper instruction, and the observance of a few simple rules.

First, silence needs to be part and parcel of our *main weekly worship*, not confined to special services at other times for those who like that kind of thing. Second, the periods of silence should be explained beforehand so that it does not take anyone by surprise. Third, their beginning and end should be clearly signalled – a Buddhist singing bowl is particularly good for this – so that everyone is reassured it is part of the plan. Fourth, they should be long enough to settle into but not too long – perhaps just two or three minutes each time at the outset. Fifth, it is the president who should give the signals before and after silence, as the person most in tune with the mood of the moment, and best equipped to withstand the urge to end silence as soon as it has begun.

---

65 Mark 9.6.

Silence is particularly appropriate immediately before worship begins, and within worship immediately following a significant moment or section. A period of silence following the reading of the Scriptures or, in the Eucharist following communion, provides us with a time to ponder in our hearts, unrushed, what we have heard and received, taking it quietly in, digesting it, committing to memory a particular phrase or moment, and contemplating the wonder of it all.

Timothy Radcliffe points out that all the Gospels begin in silence,[66] and that's where good worship begins, with the tentative, hesitant approach of the humble of heart, and where it ends, in the rapturous gaze of the lover reconciled to the beloved.

---

66 'All the gospels begin in silence; Luke with the astonished silence of Zechariah; Matthew with the puzzled silence of Joseph; Mark with the silence of the wilderness; and John with the plenary silence from which the Word comes.' Timothy Radcliffe, in Keith F. Pecklers (ed.), *Liturgy in a Post-Modern World*, 2003, p. 138.

13

Newness

New ev'ry morning is the love
our wak'ning and uprising prove.

John Keble[67]

Every act of worship is a new creation. This may appear astonishing, given our human liking for routine, but each encounter with God is unique, and so by extension is each act of worship.

Keble's hymn took its cue from a verse in Lamentations, 'his mercies never come to an end; they are new every morning'.[68] Citing this text the Jewish scholar Ivan Caine observes that innovation in worship is emphasized by the rabbis of the Talmud. Faithfulness is about more than adherence to an immutable law.

It is not surprising therefore that Jesus, emerging from that tradition, laid great emphasis on newness as the essential complement to immutability in renewing his faith tradition. Among the pictures he drew of the kingdom of God was the image of a householder who 'brings out of his treasure what is new and what is old'.[69] Note the order. We assume he said it the other way round because

---

67 John Keble 1792–1866, Leader of the Tractarian Movement and author of *The Christian Year*.

68 Lamentations 3.22–23.

69 Matthew 13.52.

'ancient and modern' comes naturally to our lips, the old first. But the Gospel puts the new in pride of place.

'Old' in the context of church does not require any special pleading because we are quite capable, all on our own and completely unaided, of restricting worship into a familiar, reassuring shape, much the same week in week out. As a result worship retains very little zest or spontaneity.

Worship in fact has become something of a gold standard by which we measure sameness and predictability. When those outside the faith community have cause to quote the Bible it is invariably the Authorized Version of 1611, and any positive press for the Church usually confined to nostalgia for 1662 evensong in a country church. As far as they are concerned, nothing much has changed, and in more instances than we care to admit, they would be right.

Although the church at Ephesus was praised for its many virtues, it did not earn a clean sheet; 'but I have this against you, that you have abandoned the love you had at first'.[70] The church had evidently gone off the boil, taking its beloved – the Lord – for granted. Today, a church which goes on singing love songs to God composed one or two hundred years ago, which can not be bothered to think of something new, is like the lazy, uncaring husband who buys his wife the same card and the same present every birthday. It invites the same verdict on its level of devotion.

While it is true of course that the essential nature of worship never changes, the Judeo-Christian tradition is not a deposit of faith set in concrete, but an ever-developing story. Constant evolution is seen in this solid

---

70 Revelation 2.4.

biblical tradition; the focus of Jewish worship moving from temple to synagogue; the emergence of the Christian Way; the proclamation of the good news to Gentile as to Jew; and in our own day a recognition of other faith traditions as authentic paths to God. Robustness of faith has gone hand in hand with exploration and the embrace of new forms and fresh understanding.

In our own generation, the liturgical renewal, spanning the twentieth century and culminating in the Second Vatican Council, has represented a kind of second Reformation, in which all mainstream Churches, responding to the alienation of contemporary society from the Church as we knew it, has opened up a new era of exploration and creativity. We have discovered many practices from the primitive Christian period which had been buried beneath later accretions. Like the urban fox searching through dustbins, and the herring gull hanging out at the back door of the fish and chip shop, we adapt in order that the species may survive.

So then, faithfulness to our own evolving history requires constant adaptation and retooling. If we believe we actually have something to *say*, relevant and sharp and for our day, then we need to say it in language and forms understood by today's generation.

This is actually not as difficult as it sounds. Balancing the timeless unchanging quality of worship with the spirit of newness and spontaneity need not be beyond us, provided we know our own history of constant evolutionary change, and commit ourselves to seeing it through into our own generation.

Sometimes it is simply the mechanics of how we produce materials for worship week by week which need tinkering with. One of the downsides of the computer age is that it is all too easy for someone in the parish office to hit 'print' and out pops exactly the same service with exactly the same hymns as this time last year.

A worship team or group will help to address this problem of repetition, but here too there are dangers of getting bogged down in a decision-making process at the expense of the end result. The skill of an able leader is needed to give people a sense of genuine ownership of the project, while retaining overall responsibility for direction and purpose. It can be done; we may just have to work at it a little harder.

Yet both modern technology and an increased sense of participation should make newness in worship more easily attainable. We have the opportunity to achieve a large impact with very little. If we make it an aim to insert a little surprise in our worship every time we gather, a tweak here, a nudge there, we shall be surprised at how quickly what had grown tired and stale can be freshened up and given a spring in its step.

Because the worship 'machine' is so steady and relentless and unchanging in most churches, irrespective of tradition, the smallest sign or gesture can indicate a whole new way of seeing things.

This may consist of a *physical change* in the environment – the removal of an altar frontal to let the furniture to speak for itself, a flower arrangement is repositioned left, instead of centre, stage; or a *change of routine* – the reader using a serious-looking book at an appropriate piece of furniture instead of standing in the aisle with a leaflet, or those who preside at the altar table receiving communion last, not first; or the *insertion of something new* – a word of Scripture by way of commentary on what we are about to do liturgically; or the omission of something we have 'always done' because it has ceased to make sense.

Explanation of changes should be brief and given *after* the event, for doing is the best way of learning, and it is a kindness not to burden anxious souls with news of forthcoming disruption to the norm.

Learning a new piece of music together, possibly a chant we can learn without books and which can be threaded through an act of worship, is another good way to keep us fresh and alert. At other times, world events – war or natural disaster – will demand that we 'interrupt normal service' to focus on what is happening and determine the most effective response available to us.

What these small but significant changes, these tweakings of the norm, will require is sensitivity, creativity and a keen eye on the part of the leadership – whether individual or team – and a commitment on everyone's part to the concept of 'newness' as an essential ingredient of worship. In our hesitant endeavours to experiment and explore will we enter into fresh encounters with the God who comes to us 'new every morning'.

14

Spirit-filled

When the Holy Spirit comes upon men and women, there is new life; there is often disorder too, untidy edges. But give me this every time if otherwise I have to put up with cold, lifeless orthodoxy.[71]

Worship is not something we 'do'; it is a time when we assemble to have something done to us. At least it is a bit of both – we proposing and God disposing – an activity in which we plan liturgies and prepare sermons, but always with the proviso that we are not entirely in control.[72]

For when we gather for worship we are approaching a rendezvous with the Spirit of God, laying ourselves open to the irruption of the source of all being into our lives. We can but show up at the appointed time, offer what we have prepared, and leave the rest to God. Unlike the hero of the thriller who is instructed to show up at the rendezvous alone and after dark, we come in community, and in the full light of God's glorious new day.

Although 'Spirit-filled worship' will for some suggest a form of worship totally free of structure, and frequently interrupted by interventions 'in the name of the Lord' as evidence of that freedom, we are speaking here of the

---

71 Donald Coggan, Archbishop of Canterbury 1974–80.

72 'The human mind may devise many plans, but it is the purpose of the Lord that will be established' (Proverbs 19.21).

75

familiar order of the regular Sunday gathering, even a formal Eucharist, which is irradiated by a powerful sense of the Spirit of God.

Spirit-filled worship is, above all, that in which we quietly and gently lay ourselves open to the Spirit of God, that at every juncture of our worship there is a sense of waiting upon God, of allowing God to speak to us, to direct our path. It requires a humble receptiveness, and a rejection of that disdainful attitude sometimes shown by the mainstream towards those for whom the gifts of the Spirit described by Paul are of primary significance in their worship.[73]

Spirit-filled worship reminds us that the Holy Spirit is not a *possession* of the Church, to be called in when it thinks fit; rather the Church is possessed by the Spirit. The Holy Spirit did not retire with a pension once the last chapter of Acts was completed, but is active among us now.

If this seems a big leap from what has gone before, know that in every community of faith there will be individuals whose hearts God has touched, and who have been waiting patiently, perhaps for many years, for something to happen in terms of God breaking in upon their community. The path has been prepared, as it was for Jesus when, at his presentation in the temple, he was recognized and hailed by the faithful Simeon and Anna.[74]

Simeon 'was waiting for the consolation of Israel, and the Holy Spirit was upon him', and in our own generation there will be those who, bearing the stamp of God's Spirit, have a longing to see things move ahead and for the kingdom to break through. We will recognize in them deep faithfulness and adventurous openness to God (age

73 1 Corinthians 12.1–11.
74 Luke 1.25–38.

has nothing to do with it!), and upon such foundations is a Spirit-filled assembly built.

A community that lays itself before the Spirit of God in a conscious, intentional way can also lay itself open to the risk of discord, even disintegration. This is why order and form and dignity are just as essential as openness and spontaneity, and why strong presidency is a *sine qua non* of balanced worship. Order is vital as a protection for all against the tyranny of the few.

Much will be asked of the pastor, who bears primary responsibility for discerning and drawing forth the gifts and ministries within the Body, for channelling the energies – at times unruly – of those filled with 'new wine', and above all maintaining unity and love. In worship, the good president will need to develop skills of cutting short interruptions to the flow of worship with sensitivity but decided firmness.

At the same time (yes here's the tricky bit!), there needs to be a willingness on the part of the president to allow on occasion for interruptions to the set form, for adaptations to what was planned, or additions to the programme, when these arise from evident, heartfelt need or good old-fashioned inspiration. The leader of worship must develop and then trust his instincts in that most vital of spiritual gifts when it comes to the leading of worship – the 'discernment of the spirits'.[75]

A widespread method of keeping the door ajar for the Spirit of God is the ministry of healing. The renewal movement of the 1970s seems to have left in its wake a smattering of people everywhere, a few in almost every assembly if you look, who once witnessed something, or read something in a book they borrowed, which has

---

75 1 Corinthians 12.10.

opened up a channel of grace in their lives, and a naturalness in bringing to God obstacles to health or wholeness. Being on intimate terms with God, feeling able and entitled to pray for healing as for other spiritual gifts, now seems far more normal than it would have done 50 years ago.

Individuals such as these tend to appear out of the woodwork whenever a time for the ministry of healing is included in Sunday worship with an opportunity for sharing in the laying on of hands. It will be surprising to see how many come forward, and to find who they are.

When we speak therefore of Spirit-filled worship, we are talking not about sensational events, but a new and deep sense of awareness of the Spirit of God working through what we have; a church, an order, a structure, a weekly routine. In this we are called to a delicate balance between order and freedom, structure and spontaneity.

When traditional order and freedom in the Spirit are combined and held together in one community of worship, we have the best of all possible worlds. Our failure to hold together these complementary insights is the tragedy of our times, leading to a polarization resulting in the foundation of new churches by those grown impatient with the old order.

For now we can but listen to one another in the assembly, working quietly but purposefully to create a culture of faith and mutual trust in which we are no longer hesitant to give witness to the wonderful works of God in our own lives, and no longer surprised by the multitude of ways in which God's grace is made known, nor by the extraordinary cast of characters used by God as messengers, healers, and agents of reconciliation and peace.

A hymn written a long time before a renewal movement was thought of addresses the Spirit with the words

'Breathe on me breath of God'.[76] That is a powerful image and the hymn has remained a favourite for 150 years or so. In the final analysis what we mean by Spirit-filled worship is just that; listening to the heartbeat of God, breathing in the breath of God.

But of course we do not rest there forever. According to Mark's Gospel the Spirit *drove* Jesus into the wilderness after his baptism[77] – none of your polite 'leading' as in Matthew and Luke – and the Spirit sooner or later will get us moving too. It may not always be comfortable, but we shall know we have been in the presence of God.

---

76 Edwin Hatch 1835–89.
77 Mark 1.12.

15

Journey

And one can only ever have begun; there is no other
way to be than to be on the way.[78]

A community of faith at worship is a community going
somewhere. It is not for ever 'circling round its own air-
port',[79] but is on the move, in a forward direction, with a
purpose in mind.

If we care to define good worship by what it is not, it
is not worship that is aimless, without purpose or direction. A faith community that does not know where it is
going, or has forgotten that it is on a journey at all, has
lost a sense of sacred history, its purpose for being. It will
produce worship that is merely the constant repetition of
a folk memory, spiralling in upon itself, with only one
place to go.

The notion of the journey of the people of God is deeply
embedded in the Judeo-Christian tradition. Furthermore
it is not a journey from one permanent stronghold to
another, but the journey of a nomadic people who know
little certainty or security other than the fact that God
travels with them.

God is revealed journeying with the people of the
Covenant on the road:

78 Catherine Pickstock, *After Writing*, 1997, p. 183.
79 A favourite metaphor of my wife's colleague Euan.

I will place my dwelling in your midst, and I shall not abhor you.
And I will walk among you, and will be your God and you shall be my people.[80]

God is encountered on the road. The communal experience of the children of Israel crossing the Sinai desert, who found God's tent pitched among their own, marked the Jewish people for ever as spiritual nomads, at home everywhere and nowhere. The later construction of a magnificent temple at Jerusalem, at last providing security and stability, was eventually found to be a false trail. It was a case of back to the drawing board, and back to the road.

'A wandering Aramean was my ancestor'[81] begins the liturgical credo of the children of Israel on arrival in the promised land, and Christians are also spiritual nomads. We follow a peripatetic Teacher who had nowhere to lay his head,[82] no home to call his own, whose whole ministry was set in the context of an overarching journey up to Jerusalem, where the final act of the drama would be played out.

Our worship then, if faithful to this overriding scriptural and historical tradition, should constantly reflect our nomadic status, our awareness that we are a people on a journey, a work in progress. The Christian Scriptures hold us to the vision, reinterpreting the temple tradition and its sacrificial worship system in purely spiritual terms. Our building programme concerns Spirit-filled communities built of living stones,[83] and our worship system is

---

80 Leviticus 26.11–12.
81 Deuteronomy 26.5.
82 Matthew 8.20.
83 1 Peter 2.4–5.

presided over not by a priestly caste but by Christ himself, 'a high priest of the good things to come'.[84]

Nevertheless the Christian Church has gone in for temple building on a scale that puts the Israelites in the shade, and (at least in the liturgical churches) stubbornly clung to a language of worship – priest, altar, sanctuary – which perpetuates a cultic pattern of thought. Our desire for shelter and security trumps theological purity any day. It seems that for Christians all this temple stuff is like chocolate; it is gorgeous, and irresistible, but too much of it is bad for us.

But all is not lost. The liturgical renewal has over the last 50 years or so dragged us back to first principles. It reminds us that always for the follower of Jesus of Nazareth worship will be more akin to an encounter on the Emmaus road[85] than a high festival in the temple precincts.

Our vision is partial, and our worship takes place in structures that are provisional, makeshift, transitory. At the next bend in the road we may see more, and enter into a fuller vision, which may require us to re-evaluate much of what has gone before and begin again. Nothing is permanent or immutable, for as God's pilgrim people we cannot, by definition, ever 'arrive' in this life. We can but journey on.

The challenge for us, therefore, is that our worship should proclaim journey rather than arrival. Even in the most splendid or ancient of our buildings our worship will need to suggest that this structure may look like a temple, but is in fact a tent; that what we celebrate may sound like an endgame but is in fact an opening move. Our worship is not static, contained within itself, but dynamic and pointing to that which lies beyond.

---

84 Hebrews 9.11.
85 Luke 24.13–33.

How might we convey these dynamic insights amid so much static grandeur? How can we both remain faithful to our sacred tradition and at the same time keep ourselves supple and alert for what may lie around the corner, the next adventure on the trail? There are a couple of significant ways in which we have traditionally flagged up journey as essential to Christian worship.

First, we have laid out our buildings as a series of rooms instead of one large single room. As soon as the Christian Church was free to make architectural provision for its worship, at the beginning of the third century, its major structures tended to consist not of one building but two; a room for worship and a separate room, or baptistry, for the rites of initiation.

The separate baptistry symbolized in a visible and concrete way that the stages of the Christian journey were not merely theoretical but physical. Although separate baptistries were a rarity after the fourteenth century, the custom persisted of placing the font near the west doors of the church building, symbolizing our entrance into the Christian life. Today the liturgical renewal, in recapturing the importance of baptism, has led to a new emphasis on the baptismal font, and a cleared space around it, as the focal point of the first stage of the faith journey.

The traditional layout of the worship space proper, with its progression from nave, through the choir, to the area containing the altar table, continued the theme of journey, despite the hierarchical accretions arising from increased clericalization. At the English Reformation Thomas Cranmer attempted, with limited success, to reinterpret these divided spaces as two rooms within a single worship area, one centred on the scriptures and one on the sacrament.

The second means of proclaiming journey arises from

the first, and consists of using fully and creatively the spaces available to us in our church building to bring this concept to life. Instead of merely watching other people move (in the customary processions of clergy and choir) the whole assembly moves as one, journeying from one area of the building to the next, each area focusing on a different aspect of the worship. In a eucharistic rite for example, the assembly might move from font (penitential rite), to ambo (liturgy of the word), to altar table (eucharistic prayer and communion).

An emphasis on journey in worship is sometimes resisted in the name of those with disabilities, but not always on their behalf. Provided that every effort is made to improve access, level the internal space, and take care of one another in a natural, unforced way, no one need feel excluded. A mature assembly works together to include everyone present in the common journey, and it is heartwarming to see how spontaneously and naturally members of an assembly aware of its calling will gather others into the action. A chair will be brought forward at the right moment, an arm offered to those who are unsteady or anxious, or reassurance given that, if movement is impossible, it is fine to sit still and let others come to you.

Where there is insufficient space within the church building, or where space is too cluttered, we need to experiment with other possibilities, bringing into play other rooms or halls at our disposal, as well as the open air when weather permits. We are familiar with such 'camping out' on Palm Sunday, or when the heating breaks down in the church building, but need to build on this experience and become a little more adventurous with the regular Sunday routine.

Using both hall and church for a Sunday Eucharist for

example, celebrating word in one and sacrament in the other, does more than bring alive for us the concept of journey. It helps us learn to worship from scratch again, at least for part of the service, becoming more creative as we do without the props which we ordinarily consider essential. It also may enable the assembly to end up in the same room where coffee will be served afterwards, a practical necessity if we mean business about befriending the newcomer.

This in turn may involve several adjustments to our normal procedure; expanding our musical repertoire to include many songs or chants suitable for singing as we move, without the need for books or papers, and with a more adventurous use of percussion; and developing our readiness to change posture as required, sitting to hear the scriptures but standing to pray, and taking good care of those for whom movement is restricted.

Threaded through all our worship should be the golden thread connecting us to those who have gone before, who continue the journey home to God beyond the confines of this earthly pilgrimage. The Christian tradition has always seen worship on earth as a trailer for the big picture of worship in the heavenly places.

In particular the eucharistic meal is not only spiritual food for the present journey but for us a foretaste of the heavenly banquet. It is a very happy thing that the primary Christian image for what heaven will be like is that of a wedding reception – with Christ as bridegroom and the Church as bride[86] – and that accordingly each eucharistic celebration on earth is a kind of 'dry run' for the real thing, towards which in our worship we edge ever closer.

---

86 Revelation 19.7.

While physical constraints may limit the ways in which we follow through on all these aspects of journey, good worship will, in one way or another, always impress upon us that we do not, in the final analysis, belong here, for we 'sing the Lord's song in a foreign land'.[87] Everything around us is temporary and provisional, our building a flapping tent not a solid temple. But we go joyously and expectantly on our way, for our journey is a journey home to God. For 'here we have no lasting city, but we are looking for the city that is to come'.[88]

87 Psalm 137.4.
88 Hebrews 13.14.

16

Preaching

> What a rare and wondrous thing it is to hear good preaching! The feet of a good preacher are indeed very beautiful.[89]

Good worship is enlivened and enriched by good preaching. Although in some Christian traditions preaching dominates worship and defines the worship leader (the 'preacher man' of Hollywood Westerns), preaching in liturgical churches is an important component of worship rather than its be-all and end-all. The good sermon or homily is a jewel placed in the complementary setting of words, music, silence and prayer which together form our worship.

To be entrusted with this task is a supreme privilege for any human being, especially when it is combined with leadership of a faith community, where the message of the preacher is integral to the complete pastoral care and direction of the assembly.

What might we say are the characteristics of good preaching?

---

89 Isaiah 52.7.

Love

First there must be love. The preacher must love her people and relish the task of preaching. She will need to love the people to whom she preaches, with a longing to share with them her own delight in the good news and its power to transform lives. Her longing may at times be painful as she strives to convey the message, frustrated at times by her own inadequacy or by stubbornness of heart in her hearers.

John Donne, that passionate priest poet, said, 'True instruction is making love to the congregation.'[90] Donne was saying that to preach to or teach one's congregation is like a young man eager and anxious to win the heart of a girl, and that is not a bad image of how a preacher should win the heart of the assembly.

The preacher will pour herself into the enterprise of causing the assembly to look, listen and allow hearts and minds to be moved. The goal for the preacher of course is surrender to God, not to her! Through all this it is the preacher's *love* for the assembly that must shine through, not any sense that she is merely performing a duty or doing a chore. That is no way to win hearts.

As love grows between preacher and hearers, so will an eagerness to listen and a willingness to give her the benefit of the doubt. Where there is love, misunderstanding or ill-feeling is likely to be short-lived and the message will get through unhindered. In preaching, as in so much else, love covers a multitude of sins.

---

90 John Potter and Evelyn Simpson (eds), *The Sermons of John Donne*, 1953–62, p. 35.

Truth

The preacher is required to speak the truth, proclaiming it fearlessly as far as he is able to discern it, and not a version of the truth edited and adapted for consumption by a particular group of hearers. Barbara Brown Taylor has written: 'I wish preachers did not lie so much.'[91] This may come as something of a surprise to us, but there are a couple of ways in particular in which preachers will find themselves under pressure to speak just a little less than the whole truth; a kind of semi-skimmed milk of the gospel.

First we have to face the fact that every community of faith will come to worship with certain expectations about the scope and content of the preaching they are about to hear. They will not be looking to be stretched too far beyond their comfort zones. Churches, or movements within churches, will each have an emphasis and scope of preaching appropriate to that tradition. We would not normally go to a Baptist church expecting to hear a sermon about Our Lady, or to a middle-of-the-road place expecting to be pepped up about substitutionary atonement. Congregations have certain expectations and on the whole like to have their prejudices confirmed, not questioned, by the preacher.

Second, there is a gentle conspiracy of silence at work among clergy in suppressing the full story of developments in New Testament studies and in our general knowledge of how the collection of books we call the Bible was put together. The usual diet of sermons dished up in mainstream churches give no indication of the advances in scholarship over the last hundred years that help us have more clarity about which sayings of Jesus recorded in the

---

91 Barbara Brown Taylor, *When God is Silent*, 1998.

Gospels were his own and which were the product of his close followers, and to explore more penetratingly the circumstances surrounding the conception and birth of Jesus, and his resurrection appearances.

Even so uncontroversial and self-evident a matter as the stark and puzzling differences between Jesus as portrayed in the fourth Gospel compared with the first three, is usually glossed over, rather than being addressed and explored. Not upsetting the 'little old ladies' is the usual excuse proffered for not coming clean, but ironically it is often the senior members of congregations who rush up afterwards to thank an honest preacher for making clear what they themselves had always thought but been too afraid to admit.

The general public is fascinated by these questions, as evidenced by the shelves in any bookshop, and no less are members of the faith community eager to learn and explore new insights which help make their faith more real. We insult both the intelligence and the robustness of faith of our hearers by serving up theological half-truths.

Prophecy

Good preaching will need to be, at least on occasion, courageous. One of the most neglected aspects of leadership in the Church is that of prophecy, and courageous preaching will greatly increase the chances, at least now and then, of some prophecy breaking through the staleness and predictability of worship.

There should always remain a certain degree of risk in preaching. If a preacher never loses a night's sleep before preaching, if his mouth never goes dry or his knees knock as he prepares to speak, he is never going to cut any ice as a truth-telling prophet. 'First night nerves' on Sunday mornings should never go away if we mean to take preaching seriously.

But of course the preacher must never set out to offend or confront, or to aim remarks directly at a certain section or (perish the thought) at a certain individual. The preacher can but proclaim the truth as he sees it, casting the stone into the still pool, and seeing how far the ripples spread and what they dislodge. Francie, the faithful sacristan in my training parish, used to have a good line on prophetic preaching gleaned from the revered 'Vicar Hoare'; you just proclaim the truth as you see it, and after that it's a case of 'if the cap fits, wear it'.

Power

Good preaching must also move people; move their hearts, inspire their spirit, change their minds, nudge them forward on the journey. They should not end up in the same place as when the sermon began. This means that the preacher needs to be extremely focused, resisting the many temptations along the way. These include beginning with a fascinating (and sometimes long-winded) illustrative story that takes over the sermon (leading the listener to remember the story but not the point it was illustrating), or giving too many back-up quotations, biblical references, or Greek sources. All we need is the gist, not the whole nine yards.

Food

The preacher should remember that she is issuing iron rations for the troops who will go 'over the top' on Monday morning, so what she says must be apposite and economical with words, to the point. Perhaps a single phrase will be repeated several times, threaded through the sermon like a mantra, so that the listener has something to hang on to, recall when in the bus queue or the office cafeteria.

Robert Runcie[92] always taught his students at Cuddesdon to write the kernel of the message – just a short phrase – on a small card and to keep it in front of them throughout. This one message was all they had to get across, probably repeated several times.

This key phrase was not necessarily just hard fact, some theological nugget, but could be something delightful – a line of poetry perhaps, or something to make us smile – that will feed the soul and keep us warm. The assembly will not remember the whole, and should not need to, but there should be something simple, but powerful, to chew on through the week.

Liturgical context

Good preaching is liturgical, because it is part of the whole offering of worship, and integral to the theme set forth in the appointed Scripture readings. It comments on and illuminates what we are doing together in this act of worship. It raises sights, reminding us who we are, and what our calling is under God. It points us ever onward in the pilgrimage of faith, forward to new explorations of what it is to be the people of God.

Good preaching above all aims to move the heart rather than impress the brain. A frequent problem is the college essay masquerading as a liturgical sermon, read from a full text with lots of quotes from the Greek. It may impress the tutor, but leaves the assembly cold.

---

92 Robert Runcie, Archbishop of Canterbury 1980–91.

Pastoral care

Good preaching is pastoral, and binds together homilist and assembly, priest and people into a deeper unity. Preaching in the context of the regular weekly assembly growing in mutual love and in a developing understanding of the direction of its journey, the pastor is given each week these vital few minutes in which to consolidate and affirm, to gently tend, and perhaps to correct the course a little.

It is a precious opportunity and should not lightly be delegated to others. This suggests that in a larger community of faith perhaps with several staff, the assumption that everyone takes equal turn should be questioned. This is too important a task to fall victim to the tyranny of a rota, letting loose on the assembly poor preachers for fear of giving offence.

Good preaching emerges from the community the preacher serves, and is aware of its context. It is apposite; serious when the assembly needs to be solemn, light of touch, sometimes humorous, when the mood of the moment fits the bill.

Because it springs from true pastoral care for all present in the assembly, it addresses the whole body. It neither 'entertains' young children (sometimes in a way that demeans them) to the exclusion of adults present, nor addresses adults in a way that excludes children. Good preaching is inclusive of all.

Confidence

Good preaching is assured and confident, not floundering around for a theme or a point, but overflowing with an authority that comes not from the preacher but from a humble conviction of the sacred task.

The good preacher learns early on to let go of a full written text, and to preach from the heart, having prepared well and keeping in front of him some simple headings. No preacher should ever be lost for words should they be called upon at short notice, maybe of only minutes, to speak of the things of God.

Good preaching is focused, characterized by a lean and hungry look, an economy of words rather than verbosity. It is accurate and right on the ball.

Commission

The good preacher gives a sense of preaching, not in her own strength, but as someone being used, taken over, 'possessed' even, by God. One of the most effective readers and preachers of the Scriptures I have ever known was one of the quietest and most retiring people you could meet. But when she went to the ambo and addressed the assembly it was as if she was seized by the Spirit of God. This was not in any way showy, but in a sense that here in this moment she spoke in God's name, a conviction that came from deep within herself. She became, for the moment, another person.

She always began with silence, and seemed to take an age before she spoke, either to proclaim the gospel or preach the homily. She simply took her time, looked around, and began. You could hear a pin drop. Here was an authentic dynamic encounter between word, preacher and hearer. Everyone in the room was transfixed. You almost pitied the poor homilist who followed; there was almost nothing left to say.

Assembly

Without an assembly there can be no preaching. The preacher needs hearers, not just to listen passively, but to contribute attentiveness, affirmation, response. By its reaction, the assembly completes the action of preaching.

Paul Janowiak in his book *The Holy Preaching* studies the interaction of word, preacher and assembly. It is a dialogue of three voices, each acting upon, and to some extent altering, the others. The word impinges upon the preacher, the preacher moves the assembly, and the assembly responds, and in some ways can in turn impinge upon the word, so that its meaning and significance in that assembly will be deepened or changed. For Janowiak, the assembly plays a vital role 'in shaping the sacramental presence of Christ in the word. In their role as "hearers of the word", they are like bread and wine placed upon the "table of God's Word". Without these people there is no presence.'[93]

---

93 Paul Janowiak, *The Holy Preaching*, 2000, p. 137.

17

Music

Let music not void the text of meaning, but render it fruitful.[94]

The most significant single characteristic of good worship is good music. When music accompanies worship, as it certainly should at every Sunday gathering, it will provide the biggest single indicator of who we are and where we are going. Music tells us, even on a first visit, most of what we need to know about a church in order to know where it is on its journey, and whether we will want to visit again.

The issue of music in churches is the most sensitive and controversial aspect of worship, arousing passionate responses of greater intensity than any other issue except perhaps the moving of furniture, and dealing with it positively and creatively is the trickiest of the pastor's tasks. 'Good music' in a worship context may seem a subjective and elusive concept, but there are some discernible common denominators.

---

94 St Bernard of Clairvaux, exact source unknown. Quoted by Fr Chrysogonus Waddell OCSO.

Assembly as choir

Good music begins with the assembly. It begins with theology. If we have a strong grasp of the assembly as the unified body of active participants called to make music to God, we shall want that truth made explicit.

The assembly should be helped to *enjoy* making music. Learning new music and making music together should be one of the chief ways that a worshipping community is formed. Gaps in the timetable at my old school in Birmingham were filled by the irrepressible Charlie Walker who taught a load of recalcitrant teenagers how to enjoy music making. Every parish needs a Charlie Walker to help us realize the potential we have in us, and run with it.

We glimpse this process at parish weekends, and camps, and away-days, when music is usually approached as a fun exercise using whatever we have to hand. On such occasions we are helped by an outside facilitator to try new things and to astound ourselves with what we are able to achieve. The trick is to remember all this back home, where we tend to be inhibited by age-old patterns of certain people doing certain things.

Not everyone of course is equally gifted in singing or playing, yet everyone should be made to feel they play a part. A useful model here is that of a traditional monastery, in which singing the daily Mass and the Divine Office is central to their life. Every monk sits in choir, but among them those especially gifted musically will emerge from their places to stand together in a convenient place to sing anything complicated or needing special attention, for example, the 'alleluia' before the Gospel. When finished they return to their places, indistinguishable once more from the rest of the community.

We have done a grave disservice to the theology of

the assembly by dividing off singers into a distinct and separate compartment. The Victorian development of the robed choir represented the living out of a gothic fantasy, and where it survives effectively removes singers from the main body of the assembly. It also does a disservice to the music, by traditionally placing these singers in the chancel, usually the least satisfactory place in the building in terms of acoustics.

Bishop Michael Marshall boldly commented in 1982 that 'the choirs and the organists of our day constitute a real problem and even a positive hindrance to the whole of renewal in Christian worship'.[95] Sadly nothing much has changed in 30 years.

Music as servant of the liturgy

Good music should enrich the worship of the church, not be a separate show within it. Our worship must always be the first consideration; how can music make it even better? How can music give us wings?

Sadly, the phrase 'strong musical tradition' has become code for the perpetuation of an extremely narrow understanding of music for worship, restricted by and large to classics composed before 1900, sung and performed by a privileged few, while the assembly is reduced to the role of spectator. This is a travesty of the church at worship.

The majority of professional church musicians enter the field through the organist's route. Most directors of music are highly proficient organists and the organ dominates their understanding of church music. They are trained and nurtured in maintaining a musical tradition rather than facilitating worship by the whole assembly.

---

95 Marshall, *Renewal in Worship*, p. 84.

Those professional musicians responsible for the music of our cathedrals and major parish churches in particular tend to be nurtured in the field of music rather than liturgy. This can lead to a deep disdain for anything new, tuneful or populist. The fossilization of cathedral evensong, still stuck in 1662, is a case in point. This filters down to musicians in smaller churches aiming for a higher league. Try saying the words 'John Rutter' to a classically trained music director and stand back. If a musician cannot appreciate the best of Rutter and his contemporaries, alongside Gibbons or Howells, he is not the person to lead an assembly in music making.

We can contrast these narrow attitudes with other traditions such as the Roman Catholic Church in the USA where, significantly, the professional body of church musicians is called the Association of Pastoral Musicians. They are seen as liturgists and facilitators of the assembly's participation first, and virtuosi organists second. They are there to serve and enrich the church's worship, not perpetuate their own limited definition of 'sacred music'.

What we need in our faith communities are *animateurs* of music, people with the skills to train and mobilize a disparate group of diffident worshippers to transform themselves into a participatory assembly making a joyful noise to the Lord.

How different worship might become if cathedrals, for example, made the organist position a secondary post, appointing as director of music a person who would be sufficiently versatile, both musically and in the field of multimedia technology, to serve as an energizer and coordinator of the community of faith to explore a wide range of music-making.

There's a wideness in God's hymn list

The simplest and most effective change needed to bring about good worship is the intentional inclusion of a wide range of music styles and sources, with an extensive range of instrumental support, within any one act of worship.

Now that the internet has turned the world into a village, we can access instantly music from every culture and faith tradition in the world, not to mention other churches down our street. Everything from twelfth-century plainsong to twenty-first-century electronic can be ours.

A particularly rich seam of contemporary liturgical music has emerged from the Roman Catholic tradition on both sides of the Atlantic – Stephen Dean, Bernadette Farrell, Paul Inwood, Margaret Rizza, Christopher Walker to name but a few, with Marty Haugen from the Lutheran tradition.[96] They combine memorable and theological texts with lyrical and beautiful melodies one hums all week long, yet their almost total absence from the worship of the local church in England tells a sorry tale of our stubborn refusal to embrace excellent music for worship wherever it may be found.

The resources out there are rich, enormous and breathtaking, and yet by and large the local church sticks to what it knows and likes. In so doing we despise the birthright that rightly belongs to us all.

Renewing the main Sunday gathering

The overriding priority in the renewal of the church's worship should be the transformation of the regular

---

96 Sources for this material are GIA Publications, Chicago and the Oregon Catholic Press, both distributed in the UK by Decani Music.

experience of worship at the main Sunday service each week. This act of worship should model the way forward for the whole church, that is, the way of integration not segregation.

It is easy for parishes to disguise resolute resistance to change by describing the many kinds of music employed without saying *when*. Closer inspection reveals that all the more contemporary or exploratory music is consigned to special services at times other than the main Sunday service, which remains traditional and unchanging. Any positive impression gained from reading the website is shattered upon arrival at the main Sunday gathering. Here the old culture of largely Victorian music reigns supreme.

The new initiatives exist of course, but at separate times, well out of sight or sound of the main assembly. This has two grave disadvantages. First, it suggests that participants in alternative services occupy some second-class position in the life of the church, and second, it leaves the culture of the main gathering for Sunday worship untouched. 'New' and 'old' are effectively polarized.

Singing the good news

One very good reason why the main Sunday gathering should embrace a wide variety of music styles is that it is this gathering which is the main shop window for the life of the church. This is where the majority of newcomers will begin their search.

Music is a powerful tool of evangelism; it is vital that those who come searching for new meaning and purpose in life experience on their first visit music of the highest standard and with sufficient breadth and variety to ensure something for everyone. Music, alongside welcome, are the two most significant factors in determining whether we come back for more.

On the debit side, our resistance to contemporary music is probably the single most significant factor in the young and the unchurched no longer taking us seriously as a body of belief with something to offer them.

We have seen already the impact of new 'community churches' in our culture, and their phenomenal speed of growth. Contemporary music, played to a professional standard by a whole group of musicians, is for them the *sine qua non* of worship. Those communities know full well the power of music to draw in, to keep and to sway a crowd. Music is the bedrock of their worship experience.

While those in the mainstream may react negatively to the theological package of the new community churches, and disdain what they have to offer, we also need to realize that there are crowds who consume that message hungrily because it is put across in the setting of worship which is fresh and exciting and clothed in a style of music familiar to them from everyday life.

Sabotage and subversion

Much as one may despair of those who refuse outright to countenance new music, perhaps more culpable still are those musicians who only go through the motions of introducing new music, and the clergy who look the other way when they do so.

We have all experienced a new song or hymn played on the wrong instrument (for example, on the organ while the piano sits idle), or at the wrong tempo, or sung by a reluctant choir. This is satisfactory for no one, and discourages further experimentation with new material.

To introduce new material will take quite a bit of hard work. There will need to be policy on how new music is sought out, sifted through and selected, how the assembly is to be taught new material, how often it is to be used during an introductory period, and how it will be accompanied to best effect.

Another means of dodging the issue of new music is the use of hymnody which sets new words to old familiar tunes. While some of the new words may be excellent in content (though often we will hardly notice), the fact remains that the overall effect is to leave the act of worship continuing to sound like a gathering for worship a century ago. The archaic culture of the worship remains untouched.

For all these reasons therefore, it is high time for us to rethink our whole approach to music in worship. How might we, with greater adventurousness and creativity, enliven and enrich the total experience of worship through music which matches the moment perfectly, lifting us to the very gate of heaven. The assembly, and the world peering through our window, is waiting.

18

Dignity

Grace was in all her steps, heaven in her eye,
In every gesture dignity and love.

John Milton[97]

Worship is a serious business. In the final analysis it consists of humankind, naked and needy, approaching with faltering step the unknowable mystery, longing to know and to be known. Heaven's gate is not a place where we lounge around, idly chatting, but (like any other gateway or threshold of significance in our lives) a place where we wait patiently, eagerly and anxiously, as at a border crossing into a land we long to enter but have no certainty of attaining.

A proper sense of dignity is therefore an important element of good worship, indicating that we are moving into a sphere where we are no longer in control. Dignity is an outward sign of our awareness of approaching that which is totally beyond us, totally other, totally out of reach of our contriving. Here, at times at least, we tremble, apprehension being an entirely natural response to standing on holy ground.

Without dignity our worship can all too easily slip into a casual overfamiliarity with the holy. Such casual-

---

97 John Milton 1608–74, *Paradise Lost, viii.1.488.*

ness cannot help but give the impression that we are not totally sure whether there is anyone 'out there' in dialogue with us, or that we see God as a rather tame figure whom we take for granted, like a kind old uncle nodding off in his favourite armchair in the corner, with hearing aid unplugged.

True dignity in worship, however, is always understated, suggestive always of something held in reserve (something for which the English are said to have a natural aptitude). Dignity can be elusive if we treat it as a commodity we want a lump of. It is a by-product of inner disposition of heart and mind. We cannot make it happen in an instant, but we can identify various factors which contribute towards it, and school ourselves in those attitudes and habits which nurture it.

Mindfulness

If there is one word that takes us to the heart of dignity in worship it is 'mindfulness'; that acute awareness of who we are and what we are doing, even when engaged in apparently familiar or routine tasks.

The story is told of the Buddha being asked what he and his disciples did. The Buddha replied, 'We sit, we walk and we eat.' When the questioner remonstrated that this is what everyone did, the Buddha replied, 'When we sit, we *know* we are sitting. When we walk, we *know* we are walking. When we eat, we *know* we are eating.'

Thich Nhat Hahn, in relating this story, comments that 'mindfulness is very much like the Holy Spirit', and adds, 'When we are mindful, touching deeply the present moment, we can see and listen deeply, and the fruits are always understanding, acceptance, love.'[98]

---

98 Thich Nhat Hanh, *Living Buddha, Living Christ*, 1997, p. 14.

Mindfulness in worship means that we become acutely, at times painfully, aware of the texture, the colour, the sound, the silence, of the assembly, and of God's presence in the midst of it. We realize, fully, deeply and humbly, who we are. We discern the body.[99]

Because mindfulness includes attention to what is going on right now, rather than before or after, all this is revealed to us in the total uniqueness of this single present moment, not the previous one to which we look back with regret or nostalgia, nor the one to come to which we look forward eagerly or in dread. On the wings of such mindfulness is dignity borne.

Conversely, therefore, worship that lacks dignity may be defined as that which exhibits an unawareness of the situation in which we are involved; a failure to discern the true character of the gathering, the sacred nature of its task, and wondrous potential of the 'now', what Jean Pierre de Caussade called 'the sacrament of the present moment'.[100]

Silence

Dignified worship is laid on a bed of silence. It emerges from silent preparation, is interspersed with periods of silence, and draws us to silent wonder.

Pace

The pace of dignified worship is slow and steady, not rushed or frantic. Whatever the different moods or tempo within it, it will suggest that we have all the time in the

---

99 1 Corinthians 11.29.

100 Jean Pierre de Caussade 1675–1751, Jesuit mystic.

world, because there is nothing more important we can be doing. Movement is never hurried, no matter how urgent the moment.

Shape

Dignified worship will, however, have shape and purpose. It may seem unhurried and timeless, but will nevertheless by guided carefully by unseen hands. It may suggest it could go on for ever, but will be quite carefully timed.

Dress

Appropriate dress will underscore any attempt to establish a sense of dignity in worship. A clearly understood dress code for leaders and assistants needs to be established and adhered to, and time taken in the sacristy before worship to ensure that all taking part pass muster.

Leaders and assistants should take care to appear as a team rather than a collection of individuals. Attention to detail in dress is not fussiness, but an important ingredient of dignified worship because sloppiness or eccentricity in dress draws attention away from the worship to the individual.

Presidency

Dignified worship takes its cue from the president. The good president contributes preparedness, professionalism, appearance and deportment, and requires these things of all other liturgical ministers alongside.

The president allows sufficient time to prepare to lead worship so that she is never taken by surprise and has everything she needs at the right time in the right place. In particular, when addressing the assembly she should do so from an appropriate service book, designed for the purpose, held for her or placed on a lectern. She should know by heart the core texts and the link passages framing each phase of worship. Clutching a leaflet to lead the Lord's Prayer, for example, suggests plain incompetence.

The president is responsible for ensuring also that the worship never becomes either precious or oppressive. When things go wrong he will find time always for a smile of encouragement, a helping hand, but never in such a way that intrudes showily upon the common purpose. A lightness of touch, and a sense of humour, are also ingredients of dignified worship.

Signs of reverence

Views as to what is appropriate in showing reverence change over time, and the substitution of the deep bow for a genuflection is one example arising from the liturgical renewal. Local customs vary, but finding appropriate ways to honour what is important to us will be an integral part of dignified worship.

The assembly may be honoured by the exchange of deep bows between president and assembly as worship begins; the Scriptures by reaching out to touch the Gospel book when it is brought through the assembly; the altar table and what it carries by a deep bow before and after receiving communion.

Worthy artefacts

Noble simplicity should be the watchword of dignified worship, and only the best will do. 'The climate (of worship) is one of awe, mystery, wonder, reverence, thanksgiving and praise. So it cannot be satisfied with anything less than the beautiful.'[101]

If the Gospel is to be proclaimed from the midst of the assembly, the Gospel book should be of a size and weight and quality to lend solemnity to the liturgical action. Those addressing the assembly need to use the appropriate book, designed for the purpose, either at a lectern or held for them.

Candlesticks, cruets, altar linen, bread and wine, need all to be carefully selected to ensure appropriateness. Everything used must clearly serve the worship, and be 'capable of bearing the weight of mystery',[102] which the worship expresses.

Re-evaluation

Dignified worship is an evolving thing and not static or immutable. There are places where worship is carefully done and perfectly correct but which has over time, for one reason or another, become drained of life and meaning. The sense of encountering the mystery has been replaced with that of performing the rituals, going through the motions for old times' sake.

We need therefore to be constantly evaluating worship, making sure that 'what we have always done' continues to hold relevance and meaning for our own day. Building

---

101 'Environment and Art in Catholic Worship' 2.34, United States Catholic Conference 1978.

102 Ibid 1.21.

on these insights we can go on with confidence to develop new forms of reverent and dignified worship as and when needed.

All these factors will help us towards a renewed sense of dignity in worship indicative of our awareness that it is God before whom we stand as members of the holy assembly. When we come to worship we should know we have arrived at a doorway into a further world, a deeper reality, a place where we pause, awestruck, and take off our shoes to walk on holy ground.

The liturgical renewal of the last five decades or so has led to a rediscovery of the primacy of the assembly, and to a realization that dignity inheres not on a distant cloud but here in our midst. Here is the true mystery; the bread broken, the assembly healed, God-with-us Emmanuel, I AM whose tent was pitched among God's people, right there on the road with us. Here in this place is our sense of reverence and dignity reborn.

> Here in this place, new light is streaming,
>   now is the darkness vanished away.
> See, in this space, our fears and our dreaming,
>   brought here to you in the light of this day.
> Gather us in the lost and forsaken,
>   gather us in the blind and the lame;
> Call to us now and we shall awaken,
>   We shall arise at the sound of our name.
>
> Marty Haugen

19

Order

But all things should be done decently and in order.[103]

The way good worship is offered conveys that we know what we are doing and that, whatever the variables provided by different components, we operate within a given framework. This overall structure gives us shape and a sense of order and stability.

This is particularly true of eucharistic worship of course, but over a relatively short period of time any community of worship will tend to fall into a regular pattern of how it does things, and of what follows what. We are creatures of habit and are reassured by knowing what comes next, or at least having a general idea.

The framework needs only to be minimal to serve its purpose. To take the Eucharist as an example, there is little that need be fixed about it save for the very basic pattern in which we assemble in God's name, proclaim and respond to the Scriptures, make intercession, exchange the Peace, prepare the table, offer thanksgiving over bread and wine, break bread and share the gifts of God.[104]

---

103 1 Corinthians 14.40.

104 The boldest two pages of the Episcopal Church's new Prayer Book of 1979 were those setting out a pattern of eucharistic celebration using section headings only, very much in the spirit of the early Church. Sadly the attached rubric specified that this rite was 'not intended for use at the

Within that framework, the bulk of the words spoken this week will be different from those used last week. Not only the obvious variables of readings, prayers, homily and songs, but also (thanks to the richness of our current worship resources) the words of the penitential rite, the affirmation of faith, and the eucharistic prayer.

Despite our new-found freedom in the choice of texts and music, perhaps even because of it, the order and pattern of events within our worship attain an even greater significance. The basic shape of our worship will give us the security of the familiar, something to relax into, within which we can learn greater boldness to experiment, explore and extemporize.

Order is the partner of freedom, not the enemy of it. Just as the familiar pattern of what a human family 'always do' when it gathers for Christmas Day will release us from too much decision-making and free us to be truly ourselves, so order in worship enables the assembly to be truly itself, happy to be home, at ease and fully in the moment. If we know Christmas dinner is going to be served at around 3 pm, then everything else will take shape around it. Shocks and surprises and things we have never done before – even awkward moments – may occur but they will be incorporated into the day, because we have a basic plan. So it is with worship.

In ordered worship, each component should be clearly seen as part of an overall plan. Section should follow section in logical sequence, linked by introductory words which are adequate but do not interrupt the flow (no, we do not need to know the number or name of the eucharistic prayer, we need to *pray* it). There should be a unity of parts, a relationship between the various components of

principal Sunday or weekday celebration of the Holy Eucharist'. Book of Common Prayer 1979, pp. 400–1.

Scripture, music, spoken word, silence and ritual action. All should relate to the given seasonal theme that under-girds all.

Developments in liturgical renewal over the last 50 years have meant that the basic framework of the Eucharist is shared by all the major liturgical churches. Not only has a common shape of the Eucharist emerged, but advances such as the Revised Common Lectionary mean that the readings are in almost every case identical too.

This makes it increasingly difficult for the innocent bystander attending worship to determine the 'label' of any particular church community. Possibly only the announcements at the end will give the game away, which is a thoroughly healthy ecumenical development, even if it does give the ecclesiastical authorities (at least in certain quarters) sleepless nights. A common order of worship may in the end provide the ecumenical breakthrough which has as yet eluded the official negotiators, as people at the grass roots try in vain to 'spot the difference' and draw their own conclusions.

As with so many of the characteristics of good worship, much depends on the president, who must keep before her a clear picture of the whole, not allowing any one section to disturb the balance.

Without a firm and experienced hand on the tiller, the shape of our worship can easily collapse into a soggy lump of dough. The president needs to instruct clearly, to co-ordinate skilfully, and to remain in charge. Nowhere is this more important than at the communion, a point in any eucharistic celebration when the whole action can get bent out of shape. The communion can fall victim to the customs and prejudices of both worship leader and the assembly.

Customs can reveal attitudes inappropriate for the

people of God which need to be firmly addressed: leaders
and assistants receiving communion ahead of the assembly,
indicating a sense of privilege; a congregation insisting on
kneeling to receive, or receiving by intinction, indicating
a sense of communion as a private devotion, unmindful
of the whole body. These customs are both theologically
unhelpful and disruptive to the sense of order in worship.
In addition they cause delay.

Ordered worship flows from a clear sense of who we
are and what we are doing. Those who preside will do
so fully aware that true authority resides in putting self
last and in 'laying down one's life for the sheep'.[105] Those
who form the assembly do so fully aware that they are
God's beloved, 'ransomed, healed, restored, forgiven',[106]
a community come of age. No longer do they grovel in
unworthiness, but with joy know themselves to be the
sons and daughters of God, bold enough to pray the
prayer that Jesus taught us and to 'stand in your presence
and serve you'.[107]

Posture and custom flow from these essential insights.
President and assembly bow to one another at the
beginning of worship to show their mutual respect and
interdependence; those who lead worship place themselves
in the circle of participants and receive communion last;
those who form the assembly exhibit their understanding
of the shared priestly life by praying together standing,
heads erect and hands open and extended, ready to assist
one another in sharing communion around the altar table

---

105 John 10.11.
106 Praise my soul, the King of Heaven!
    To his feet thy tribute bring;
    ransomed, healed, restored, forgiven,
    who like me his praise should sing?
        Henry Francis Lyte 1793–1847
107 *Common Worship* 2000, *Eucharistic Prayer B*.

in the midst, rather than kneeling at a distant altar rail.

Good worship has about it a strong sense of order, uniting us with the communities of faith which stand alongside us, across time over the last 2,000 years, and across the world today, having the same intention, using the same framework. Here we are given a clearer understanding of the whole action of liturgical worship and of our part in it.

Order frees us from any requirement to 'invent' worship all over again, but instead to slot into a given liturgical structure our own images of God, our own acts of love and praise, and the insights of our own generation.

20

Authenticity

Nothing which pretends to be other than it is has a place in celebration, whether it is a person, cup, table or sculpture.[108]

Good worship has about it an innate authenticity. It rings true. Many problems in the ordering of worship spring from our failure to stop and think what we are doing, and to ask ourselves what it says to others. We tend to go on doing what we have always done, because that is what we know and are happy and familiar with. The call of Jesus is, however, more demanding and challenging than an invitation to endless and mindless repetition.

Our task is to examine each component of worship, to consider afresh its purpose, and to determine whether the way in which we carry it out is 'fit for purpose', that is, worthy of God and of God's people. If we carry out this task faithfully, good worship will design itself, flowing from our clear understanding of who we are and what we are doing.

A clear sign that this process is taking root is when we are able not only to recognize worship that speaks powerfully to us, but to go on from there to make it our own, applying what we have observed to our own situation and creating appropriate rituals of our own.

---

108 'Environment and Art in Catholic Worship', 2.36.

Paul and Lara were a young couple who had come to appreciate at our Sunday gathering in Philadelphia the use of water at the penitential rite, and the assembly's gathering around the baptismal font at the beginning of every Eucharist. They liked the invitation to members of the assembly to go forward, touch the water, and mark the forehead of a neighbour with the sign of the cross as a sign of reconciliation.

On their wedding day Paul and Lara asked to appropriate this simple ritual within their wedding ceremony, making the baptismal font one of the foci of this ritual commitment to one another. This had never been done before; no one suggested it to them. They made the connection and adopted this ritual act for their own big day, because worship had been real to them in that place.

The process requires that we think *theologically*. We need to take each action within our worship and ask ourselves whether what we do expresses sufficiently clearly our picture of God, and of our assembly as we wish it to be. Where we feel our customary approach is lacking we need then to explore ways of demonstrating what is important to us.

A prime example is making explicit the nature of the assembly as a priestly community. This is a key feature of authentic worship, especially in the context of the Eucharist. Taking Scripture and tradition as our guides, how might we fashion worship to articulate more clearly who we are as an assembly gathered by God?

As we have seen, the rediscovery of the assembly as a royal priesthood and holy nation, and of the baptismal community as the minister of the Eucharist, are crucial aspects of the liturgical renewal of the last 50 years or so. Our task in worship is to make sure that these insights do not remain dry theory but are translated into actuality every time we gather.

One way of achieving this is to invite all the members of the assembly to adopt the same postures as the president, chiefly the *orans* position of prayer, standing erect with hands raised and open. This posture, purloined over time by the ordained leader, originally belonged to all God's people at worship.

Inviting the assembly to adopt this posture for the whole eucharistic prayer, and possibly at other points such as the prayer of the day, makes visible and tangible the theology of the baptismal community. Where the assembly can physically gather around the altar table this becomes an even more powerful sign, and for good measure the president can take a step back from the table and take up a position within the circle.

Before the eucharistic prayer begins, when the gifts have been offered at the altar table, a potent sign of the assembly's active role in the proceedings is for all present to be invited to offer themselves also, as a living sacrifice in response to Paul's exhortation.[109] As they do so they might repeat gently and prayerfully a song of offering such as John Bell's 'Take O take me as I am', or Margaret Rizza's 'Silent, surrendered'.

In places where incense is used, a further way of honouring the assembly is for the president, instead of delegating the censing of the people to a server as is customary, to cense each person in the assembly gathered around the altar table, slowly and solemnly. For this is a community of holy people for whom God has prepared holy gifts.

Individual members of the assembly may be honoured and affirmed when undertaking roles on behalf of the

---

109 Romans 12.1.

whole community. One way of doing this is for those who address the assembly at various points in the liturgy – readers, intercessor, preacher – to first come forward to the president and, after the exchange of bows, be vested in the president's stole (not a spare stole lying around) as a sign of shared authority. Even those who have been reading for years speak powerfully of the difference this simple act makes; they feel recognized and empowered.

'Careless talk costs lives' was a World War Two security slogan, and careless talk in liturgy may cost us thinking people who seek authenticity. If, for example, we have passed beyond the notion of God as an old man with a beard in the sky, then we should make sure that what we say in worship is of a piece with our thinking. 'Glory be to the Father . . .' may be hallowed by time and custom, but it essentially limits our vision of God's wondrous being. New forms that both honour God and respect human-kind's new and deeper understanding may serve us better. Here's one example: 'Glory to God, source of all being, eternal word and living spirit; the God who is, who was, and who will be, for ages unending. Amen.'

Each community of faith will develop their own ways of emphasizing those theological insights they feel most strongly about and which move and inspire them. There is no 'right' or 'wrong' in this process, only the obligation under God to be true to self and as transparent in our words, actions, signs and rituals as we can possibly be. In so doing we shall arrive at worship which is truly authen-tic, which honours God and proclaims to the world our joy in being and belonging.

21

Structures

> According to the grace of God given to me, like a skilled master builder I laid a foundation, and someone else is building on it. Each builder must choose with care how to build on it.[110]

Those who live in community – whether student accommodation, a monastery, a commune or a family home – know that the smooth-running of all such institutions, no matter how splendid the preliminary concept, will in the end boil down to whose turn it is to change the bag in the kitchen bin.

A community that worships together will face the same challenge of practical detail. A renewed vision of what it means to be an assembly will remain theoretical if we do not pay attention to how our Sunday gathering actually *works*. Who exactly makes it happen? Whose job is it to do what? How can we arrange things so that everybody gets a turn and accepts responsibility?

The interrelatedness of the whole body at worship may come as a surprise in some quarters.

'I wasn't ordained to do the washing up!' a curate once famously declared, and we hear of cathedrals where people 'come for the music' but where no one is willing to help serve coffee afterwards.

---

110 1 Corinthians 3.10.

Such attitudes arise from a deep-seated privatization of worship, the reduction of corporate worship to a private arrangement between the individual and God. Worship is seen as being made for the individual, rather than the individual for worship. The first question for many worshippers, like Britons regarding the European Union, is 'What's in it for me?' To misquote J. F. Kennedy, we should not ask 'what can worship do for me?' but 'what can I do for worship?'

A second factor limiting participation in worship is collusion. Wherever a pastor reluctant to delegate or disinclined to reorganize coincides with a passive congregation accustomed to letting a few people run the show, you have a marriage made in heaven. It is an easy way out for both parties but one which restricts and delays the community's growth into maturity.

This situation can be further exacerbated by the various cliques and interest groups ready to fill the power vacuum in such a climate, clutching tightly the reins of various components of worship whether readers, sacristans, or flower arrangers, jealously guarding their traditional roles and keeping newcomers at bay.

If all that were not enough, we find a further obstacle to full and active participation in the insidious clericalism that lurks everywhere in organized religion. The hierarchical layout of our traditional worship spaces is matched by our innate tendency to offload onto others certain roles in the assembly which should be the responsibility of us all. Where possible we like to dress them up in special clothes and park them in special seats, moving them up (literally) a step or two in the worship space, in the hope that they will 'do the God business' on our behalf, allowing us to slumber on.

Overcoming this fragmentation and polarization in the ministry of the local church should be a top priority of those concerned to reawaken our sense of worship as the work of the people of God.

One good way of achieving this is to form teams of ministry which cut across previously defended boundaries of responsibility. In this approach, the assembly is subdivided not into specialist groups – readers, intercessors, altar servers, etc. – but into mixed teams, each one of which is designed to include the various gifts and ministries necessary to make worship happen.

So, for example, the existing cohort of readers in a parish would be disbanded as a separate group, and its members dispersed in equal numbers to the new teams. Likewise with intercessors, servers, greeters and coffee-makers and every other necessary role. In this way each team will end up with a portion of the expertise in all the tasks integral to the experience of Sunday worship.

On a particular Sunday therefore, one of the teams will be assigned to duty, and will be responsible for all aspects of worship other than those fulfilled by the worship leaders and by the music team. This will include both the *support ministries* – the preparation of the room, the greeting of worshippers at the door, the ministry of hospitality, and clearing and tidying the room – as well as the *liturgical ministries* such as reading, leading the prayers, bringing forward the gifts, etc.

The number of teams will depend on the size of the congregation, but each should be large enough to offer a variety of gifts – say at least 15 strong – but small enough to maintain a close sense of fellowship. The question of frequency of duty is also an important factor. Four teams, each on duty once a month, is an absolute minimum if people are not to feel overstretched. Conversely, with any more than 12 the gaps between duty Sundays may well be too long.

If teams can be organized on a geographical basis, so much the better. This will then encourage the habit of getting together quite naturally to plan and organize, and will assist in the process whereby a ministry team gradually takes on, in addition to its primary task of facilitating worship, the role more familiar to us in the house group, where people gather to pray together, widen understanding and share a meal. Here Christian formation can occur in depth.

Leadership is of course a crucial factor in the effectiveness of such teams. The leaders need to be hand-picked by those responsible for the care of the whole community, and be respected and trusted members of the assembly. They need to be not only good organizers and co-ordinators, but gifted in the ministry of encouragement as well as being able to follow up sensitively but firmly those who let others down (for example, the family who undertake to take care of hospitality next Sunday but who arrive with big smiles but empty hands).

The role of the team leaders (and there may be more than one for each team) means that they become in effect co-pastors with the clergy, providing a ready-made structure of pastoral oversight.

This in turn means that their own pastoral care, and training, by the ordained leadership is of the highest importance. A monthly meeting of clergy and team leaders provides an exceptionally effective means of combining a time of formation for team leaders with the discussion of pastoral concerns and of forward planning for the whole community. In other words, the leaders learn on the job. To top it all, this approach provides a model of leadership largely free from the stultifying

effects of clericalism, being organic rather than hier-
archic.

Without some such structure – and the beauty of what
is suggested here is that it is endlessly variable depending
on local circumstances – worship can so easily slip back
into something done for us instead of by us. Whenever
this happens we miss the point of why we have gathered
together in the first place. We forget whose turn it was to
empty the bin.

When we commit ourselves to work intentionally
at developing appropriate structures for the real and
effective sharing of tasks and ministries in our Sunday
assembly, the impact on our common life is remarkable.
In so doing, we work towards the vision of an assembly as a true community of gifts and ministries and grow
steadily in appreciation of one another and in delight at
the blossoming of the people of God.

22

Formation

Do not be conformed to this world, but be transformed by the renewing of your minds, so that you may discern what is the will of God – what is good and acceptable and perfect.[111]

We sometimes suppose worship to be the end-product of the Christian life, the final box ticked after all the others have been squared away. It is as if we stagger into worship for rest and refreshment after a hard week escorting old ladies across the road, being nice to nasty people, and signing up for yet another sponsored walk. In this scheme of things, worship closes the deal.

In fact it is the other way round. Worship is the formative experience which shapes our Christian response to the world around us, which fires up our engines as catalysts of change and transformation. It is our first port of call rather than the last.

Participatory worship (rather than observed worship) is the first and best means of spiritual formation because when we enter fully into an act of worship the whole Christian story is not only recapitulated and set before us, it becomes ours. The Eucharist, by its very nature and the balance of its constituent parts, is the pre-eminent, though not the exclusive, example of this process.

111 Romans 12.2.

Every time we enter fully and unreservedly into the worship, 'with hearts and hands and voices',[112] allowing ourselves to be caught up in the action, we are taken into the heart of the timeless story of God's creation, and rescue, of humankind; we enter into the mystery.

Participation in worship has always seemed to me the supreme way of incorporation into the Christian community of faith, whatever our stage on the journey. The younger members of our communities deserve the best in terms of withdrawal classes and special facilities, but they also deserve the very best of worship, full of colour, movement and tactility, and providing them with a real sense of involvement.

Likewise those seeking a church wedding or baptism for a child should be given not only instruction and guidance, but, above all, a glimpse of worship at its very best. If they can experience at least for a period of time the joy of participatory worship, this is what they will carry with them years hence, rather than the discussion in the pastor's office. Where participation in worship is presented as the most important segment of preparation, the ceremony itself will no longer entail a visit to a strange and alien place, but instead a coming home to familiar territory and a house of friends.

Worship *is* formation, and is so at many levels. First, the dedication required to set aside regularly one morning a week involves a not inconsiderable feat of swimming against the tide. As we gather week after week for worship we place ourselves very definitely in a minority interest, and in this very act of standing aside intentionally from

---

112 Now thank we all our God,
   With hearts and hands and voices.
   Martin Rinkart 1586–1649

the bulk of the population we gradually awaken to the fact that we are marked men and women; the people of God. Such standing apart from the madding crowd inevitably helps form our spiritual character.

Second, we are formed by interaction with each other as fellow members of the Body of Christ. We both delight and irritate one another. We give each other hope for humankind, and at times cause to despair of it. We shall be enthralled and invigorated by one another's company, and at the same time have all those awkward corners knocked off us, or rather, rubbed slowly away.

Third, the impact of what we hear and say and do and handle shapes and moulds us. Our immersion in the Scriptures, our singing of the psalms, our movement together to gather round the foci of worship – font, or ambo or altar table – our standing together, shoulder to shoulder with hands uplifted, to offer praise and thanksgiving, our handling holy things, our tasting of the good things of God, our awed silence.

Finally, the gift of new purpose, the renewed sense of commissioning as agents of transformation, the eagerness to be out there doing something, are all reawakened by participation in good worship. Authentic worship does not leave us where we were, but moves us forward to a place where we are changed, moved, touched, redirected.

Worship alone of course is not the whole story of spiritual formation, but it is the centrepiece. A comprehensive programme of formation will embrace a wide variety of activities which may include:

- Sunday instruction classes for all age groups (not just children). Once a scattered community is gathered for Sunday worship it makes sense to extend the time to include opportunities for learning and socializing. Worship, meal and instruction are a good mix, in whatever order.

- The weekly small group meetings in the home, for prayer, study and fellowship, which strengthen the cellular structure of the church and which provide a 'shallow end' for the newcomer.
- The annual opportunities provided by a parish weekend, retreat, pilgrimage, parish holiday or summer camp.
- Opportunities for shared practical tasks and projects.

But all these spring from an experience of participatory worship, and are sustained by it. While we can envisage Sunday worship without these other complementary aspects of formation, these activities divorced from Sunday worship would lead eventually to individualistic separation from the main stream of God's love and activity among us.

It is supremely in worship that our minds are renewed and our hearts 'strangely warmed'[113] as we work joyously together to embrace in community that which is good, and acceptable, and perfect.

---

113 The phrase used by John Wesley to describe his conversion experience on 24 May 1738 during a meeting of a religious society in Aldersgate Street, London.

PART 4

A Worship Checklist

Setting

The room

The room, even empty of people, should speak clearly of the things of God, and of the nature and purpose of the assembly that gathers here. Take time to look with fresh eyes at the room you have.

- Make an inventory of everything in the room, and remove anything that no longer serves any purpose or was last used more than ten years ago.
- Reduce clutter and eradicate duplicate symbols and objects.
- Allow simplicity to focus our attention and to speak through our busyness and fussiness.
- Be bold; this is missionary work.

The seating

Let the seating plan of the room speak clearly of who you are.

- Appropriate for a community of faith, a gathering of ministers, not a collection of individuals.
- Arranged around the foci of worship, not lined up in front of them, as in a lecture hall.

- Let everything articulate full and active participation.
- Let the seating be sufficient for, not surplus to, regular requirements.

Liturgical furniture

Liturgical furniture – the objects which focus attention on different aspects of worship – should be so arranged that they maximize a sense of communal participation.

- Provide generous space around each liturgical foci – ambo, altar table, font.
- Let each become the focus of a 'room within a room', holding up before the assembly a particular aspect of worship.
- Avoid lining them up on a 'stage' at one end of the room.
- Allow the baptismal font special prominence and space, to offset previous marginalization.

Welcome

'ALL are welcome.' Which bit of the word 'all' did you fail to understand?

Bishop Rodney Michel, Acting Bishop of
Pennsylvania 2010

Training

Who are those nervous-looking people hanging around by the church door, unsure and uncertain? Are they new-comers, or your welcome team?

- Honour this ministry of welcome, within the church, recruiting those with a gift for befriending.
- Provide proper training for the welcome team.

- Understand welcome and hospitality as process not event, i.e. it ends only when the last person has gone home.
- Appoint as leader of this team someone capable of exercising a key pastoral role in the life of the church.
- Monitor effectiveness. Set up a monitoring process to assess who is best suited to this 'first contact' ministry (welcomers who talk to each other rather than the newcomer will have a negative impact).

Simplify

- Reduce to a minimum the number of different things handed out at the door. This is an evangelistic decision with an ecological dimension.
- Reduce to a minimum the worship texts supplied to each worshipper. If we are paying attention we do not need every word replicated in front of us.
- Provide everything the worshipper needs, including music, on a service sheet (possibly seasonal).
- Use overhead projection where appropriate and practical, for worship texts, preaching and imagery.

Take a real interest

When we welcome a newcomer to worship, we are saying hello to someone whom we hope may become a member of our community.

- Be warm and personal.
- Give your own name (and wear a name tag) and learn theirs.
- Offer the newcomer a temporary name badge.
- Keep an eye on those you welcome for the first time, ready to help or guide throughout worship.

- Develop a natural curiosity about those who come. Where are they from? What brought them?
- Make connections between newcomers and regulars with whom they have something in common; same street, similar job.
- Discern genuine need, whether practical or spiritual, and make the connection to the right person or resource.

Environment

Give proper consideration to the environment of welcome, the visitor's first impression.

- Create sufficient space around the entrance to avoid crowding and congestion.
- Separate where possible the welcome zone from the worship room.
- Invest in good materials for display, information and storage.
- Keep information up to date.

Music

Assembly as choir

The whole people of God is called to make a joyful noise to the Lord.

- The director of music should relate primarily to the assembly and secondarily to the specialists within it.
- Every Sunday assembly should include a time when all present practise new music.
- The whole assembly should be encouraged to join in part-singing, but from memory.

- Emphasis should be laid on learning refrains, chants, songs and choruses that can be threaded through worship without recourse to the printed word, and sometimes unaccompanied.
- Every effort should be made to make rehearsal times a fun experience.
- Use an outside facilitator from time to time to teach new techniques or new music.

Specialists as helpers

In every faith community there will be those specially gifted in voice or with instruments who can enliven and sharpen up the offering of the whole body.

- Those with special gifts – singers and musicians – should be nurtured and trained in a ministry of supporting and enriching worship.
- Singers and instrumentalists are part of the assembly and should be seated among everyone else, emerging from their places as needed.
- They should not be distinguished from the rest of the assembly by distinctive robes.
- When the singers emerge to present a special piece of music they should stand alongside rather than 'up front' in performance mode.

World music

- The musical repertoire of the assembly should be drawn from as wide as possible a range of resources, both ecumenical and international, both contemporary and from centuries ago.
- Music for worship should be provided in orders of

service, or where appropriate by overhead projection, rather than hymnals.

- At any one service it should be a matter of policy to include something new and something old, something never heard before and something evergreen, something from one's own tradition and something from someone else's.

Appropriateness

A frequent problem with music making for worship is the temptation to live beyond our means. Little country churches try to be big suburban churches, and big suburban churches try to be cathedrals.

- Take stock of where you are, who you are, and what resources you have available. Forget what other places do; what suits you?
- Avoid dependency on any one instrument or any one musician. Broaden the range of instruments to accompany song; for example, a piano and electric piano in addition to organ.
- For each piece of music, take time to select the appropriate instrument.
- Explore options for recorded music and systems to support song with recorded accompaniment.
- When new songs are introduced, ensure appropriate accompaniment from day one, or delay introduction.

Beginning

Help the assembly to embrace a common vision of what worship is about, that all may contribute to making it special.

- Ring the changes with entrance choreography. Sometimes a quiet gentle opening is required, with the leadership emerging from the assembly. On other more festive occasions a 'grand entrance' will fit the bill, with music and banners and torches.
- Help the assembly to embrace a common vision of what worship is about, that all may contribute to making it special.
- Begin as you mean to go on. Let the leader's first word set the tone for all that follows.
- Don't drift into worship, but launch it with élan, with a sense of occasion.
- Let the extempore words of welcome be either before or after the solemn greeting or invocation, not the substitute for it.

Saying sorry

Making a communal act of saying sorry to God is a challenge, for any assembly is a collection of individuals each coming to worship in a different state of mind.

- Make every effort to avoid 'vain repetition', unchanging week in, week out.
- Use a wide variety of texts, both from the alternatives provided in Common Worship and from those composed by members of the assembly.
- Use different voices from among the assembly to lead, provided that the president always introduces and concludes the rite.
- Where possible invite the assembly to gather around the font where their faith journey began.
- Explore ways in which we can say sorry in simple rituals as well as words.

- Make use of water as a powerful symbol of cleansing and renewal.
- The president might sprinkle the assembly with water from the font.
- Members of the assembly might be invited to come forward to the font, dip their fingers in the water, and sign another with the baptismal sign of the cross as a token of reconciliation and new beginning.
- Other rituals might include the writing of sins on pieces of paper and burned in a brazier, or the placing of small stones placed around the foot of a large cross.
- Music should be used creatively in the penitential rite. Some of the most beautiful and haunting contemporary music for worship is written around the theme of water and renewal of baptismal life.

Opening prayer

The way the opening prayer is said or sung sets the tone for all that follows.

- Look as if you mean business and have come prepared. The prayer should be read or intoned, not from a leaflet, but from an altar book which carries weight, literally and figuratively.
- Stand in a pivotal position in relation to the assembly, as the responsible person who calls the meeting to order and addresses the gathering with significant words.
- Slow down. Let there be a L O N G pause between the invitation 'Let us pray' and the praying.
- Say or sing the prayer with heart, slowly and purposefully, yet with a quickening pace at the climax of the prayer.

- Be choosy about texts, and dig around. Choose prayers that relate strongly to the themes of the Church's year or to the particular cycle of readings. Take a look at *Opening Prayers: Collects in Contemporary Language* or *Prayers for an Inclusive Church*, both by Canterbury Press.

The readings

The reading of the Scriptures in the assembly is a grace-filled dialogue between God and humankind.

- Honour the Scriptures. Lift them up in the midst of the assembly, prominently displayed as people enter the room, and during worship.
- Sharpen focus on the Scriptures by having them read and preached from the same prominent piece of liturgical furniture, and let this not be at one end, but in the middle, of the room.
- Those who read in the assembly should undergo preparation to understand the privilege of the role.
- Readers should be trained in posture, audibility and good reading skills.
- Reading is a ministry open to everyone willing to be trained.
- The ministry of the reader may be affirmed by him or her being vested with the stole by the president.

Psalmody

The psalms are an essential component of Christian worship for they are the songs of the Scriptures beloved of Jesus. They cover every mood in humankind's roller-coaster relationship with God.

- The psalm provided in the Eucharist should always be used, not replaced by a hymn, which impoverishes the richness of the rite.
- The psalm at the Sunday assembly should always be sung, not recited. To say, rather than sing, a psalm in worship is to subvert its purpose and dull its impact.
- The psalm should be sung in a way that enables full participation by all. For this purpose, Anglican chant is not usually appropriate.
- Explore the many alternative ways of singing the psalms by the whole assembly. Modern resources are rich and varied.
- Responsorial psalms are particularly appropriate. The settings by Gelineau never date, and offer responses learned by the congregation within minutes. Other options of more recent date abound, both responsorial and metrical versions.
- The assembly sits for the psalm, because it is a moment to savour the words and music, reflecting on the readings and our sacred history.

The Gospel

- In the Eucharist, let the book of the Gospels be carried in procession, lifted high.
- Let lights be carried to accompany the Gospel book.
- Let the Gospel be read with due solemnity and yet with a sense of excitement.
- Rehearse the assembly in making strong and joyful responses to greet and conclude the Gospel.
- Let the assembly be invited to reach out to touch the book of the Gospels as it passes near them.
- Following the Gospel (or alternatively following the homily) a period of silence should be kept for reflec-

tion, announced and concluded by a customary signal from the president, the assembly seated.

Preaching

The sermon or homily is integral to worship, but as one component among many rather than as a 'party piece' before which everything else takes second place.

- The preacher interprets what the worshipper sees and experiences, lifting the eyes of the assembly to the glory that shall be revealed among us.
- Like an experienced tour guide, the preacher provides the commentary on the journey, the landscape through which we pass, prominent features and navigation points.
- The place of preaching should be the same as that for the reading of the Scriptures, historically an ambo set in the midst of the people in the nave of the church building, understood as a table around which the assembly gathers to eat the food that is more than bread alone (Matthew 4.4).

Affirmation

It is customary in liturgical churches for the gathered assembly to include in its Sunday worship a communal affirmation of faith. Traditionally this has taken the form of a creed (Latin *credo* 'I believe') or prescribed text encapsulating orthodox belief. Forged in the heat of fourth-century religious controversy, their meaning today is not immediately obvious. But the original urge to proclaim belief stemmed from a desire to show solidarity with those being admitted into our fellowship rather than to affirm correctness.

- Explore alternatives to the Nicene or Apostles' Creed in order to avoid unthinking repetition.
- Experiment with alternative forms found in Common Worship, particularly those recapturing the ancient baptismal question and answer form, usually three-fold.
- Such return to the practice of the first three centuries chimes well with the contemporary emphasis on inclusivity, and a less doctrinaire approach to the precise nature of truth.

Intercession

Intercession is one of the components of worship with a clear New Testament warrant (1 Timothy 2.1) and is a necessary antidote to any tendency for either community or individual to be over concerned with self. In our concern for those around us we keep unity with Jesus himself, whose compassion for those in sickness or despair, and for the directionless crowd 'like sheep without a shepherd' (Matthew 9.36) was a constant feature of his ministry.

- The 'prayers of the people' should be just that; an opportunity for members of the assembly to lead the community in prayer, in their own words and their own way.
- Alternative options for the prayers of the people in modern eucharistic rites should be used as a guide not as a script.
- Every encouragement should be given to the composition of prayers by members of the assembly. Creativity should be nurtured.

- Guidance notes should be provided by the leadership team as to how to prepare and how to lead public prayer, and what to include as well as what to omit.
- Accept a degree of risk. The inclusion of a petition for the local football team is not the end of the world, and most congregations are indulgent of any shortcomings of those they see trying hard.

The Peace

The sharing of the Peace as a sign of reconciliation and mutual love within the community of faith (1 Thessalonians 5.26) is one of the most potent symbols of the rediscovery of worship as an interactive event rather than a lecture or spectacle.

- The Peace is appropriate at all sorts of worship – not just the Eucharist – whenever the occasion demands a transition from words and ideas to interactive encounter, a sealing of the bond.
- The Peace needs to be warm and natural and yet sensitive and restrained, for it speaks of the very nature of the assembly.
- We should greet those around us rather than the person we fancy greeting; the stranger rather than the old friend; those we find next to us rather than those we seek out.
- We should keep a watchful eye for those who are among us for the first time, who may feel excluded if the Peace is prolonged.
- The president should monitor the Peace as a gauge of the assembly's connectedness with itself and with others.
- Let no one be discouraged by the discomfort the Peace

occasionally provokes in some, for this is a telling sign of its efficacy.

Offering

A proper sense of the assembly's offering is essential to worship which aims at full and active participation: each participant bringing something worthy 'to the table' whether the occasion is eucharistic or not.

- Where possible, the assembly should move together, after sharing the Peace, to stand around the altar table, as co-celebrants of the sacred meal.
- Everything that is needed for the eucharistic meal should travel with the assembly; the white linen cloth, the bread, wine and oil, together with a symbol of the community's regular financial commitment.
- The gifts of bread, wine and oil should be carried by the people from a table near the entrance up to the altar table around which the assembly is gathering.
- Avoid the unfriendly custom of passing the plate.
- Offerings of money collected as people enter the room should be brought to the table with the other gifts.
- The offering of the gifts should culminate in the offering of the assembly of itself as a living sacrifice, accompanied by an appropriate song.
- Where incense is used, the president censes the assembly, the holy community offering holy gifts.

Giving thanks over bread and wine

The act of giving thanks over bread and wine, in the Jewish pattern of prayer given new power and import by Jesus, is at the heart of eucharistic worship.

- The assembly is the minister of the Eucharist.
- The president speaks on behalf of, not instead of, the assembly.
- The arrangement of the room and the position and posture of the assembly should all communicate the theological significance of this act of worship.
- The assembly should be gathered around the altar table to signify the active priestly role of the whole community.
- Members of the assembly should be invited to stand to offer this prayer, with hands open and extended in the *orans* posture of prayer.
- The president leads the assembly in the eucharistic prayer, but ways should be explored of sharing the task between several voices and the voice of the whole assembly.
- The president should lead from within the circle of the assembly around the altar table, standing back from the altar table.
- Manual acts are those shared by the whole assembly, not exclusive to the president alone.

Communion

Over the last 50 years or so the people of God have moved from 'we do not presume' to 'we thank you for counting us worthy to stand in your presence and serve you'. A sense of unworthiness has been swallowed up by a sense of joyous participation of the children of God, forgiven and redeemed.

- Arrangements for communion should assume standing, rather than kneeling, as the norm. This returns to primitive practice and recalls the instruction to the children of Israel to consume the Passover as food for the journey, with loins girded and staff in hand (Exodus 12.11).

- Altar rails should be removed. Removing visual fences and boundaries from around the altar table has a theological as well as spatial impact.
- The logistics of how communion is shared will vary from place to place and from season to season.
- Variety should be encouraged in order to break down the territorial aspects of any method of communion stultified by long custom.
- Communion in both kinds gives an opportunity to distinguish between the two in the manner of how the sacrament is shared. It is good to stress both reverent reception (for example, each member of the assembly receiving the holy bread from the hands of the president or other liturgical minister) and equal participation by the children of God (for example, each member of the assembly taking the cup into their own hands at the altar table, or passing it one to another).
- Where communion is shared by the assembly gathered standing around the altar table, the whole assembly should wait until all have received before returning to their places.
- When all have received, the assembly, at the invitation of the president, makes a deep bow of reverence.
- Methods of communion should be encouraged that take for granted the right of all members of the assembly, irrespective of age, to approach the altar table and to handle the holy gifts.
- Any method of communion is to be encouraged which renders intinction more difficult and less acceptable.

Post communion

The greater the sense of full and active participation by the assembly, the greater the awe and wonder at what has been revealed, seen and handled, in their midst. The mystery demands silence and reflection.

* Immediately following communion, the assembly should be invited by the president to return to their places and, at a given signal, enter a short time of silent reflection.
* When the silence ends (again at a given signal) appropriate music should be played of a reflective nature, preferably a contemporary eucharistic song or an appropriate piece of instrumental music.

Sending out

Worship happens in a room where the door is always ajar, not just for the latecomer, but for the world outside. In worship the assembly is reminded of the working out of the good news of Jesus in practical application, and this begins in interaction over refreshments, brimming over into the week ahead.

* Notices and housekeeping announcements come best just before the end of worship where, instead of interrupting the flow, they focus minds and hearts on the task of transformation that awaits.
* Leading members of the community should be invited to give the announcements on a rota basis, to embody shared responsibility and to vary the voices of the worship experience.
* At this point the president may feel moved to invite forward anyone who wishes to be prayed for, or blessed, by the assembly gathered around them.

- A formal blessing is theologically superfluous at a eucharistic celebration, and the formal rite should end in the sending forth (dismissal) by the deacon or other liturgical minister.

Hospitality

In both the Hebrew and Christian Scriptures the offering of hospitality is crucial to the understanding of how we encounter God. Hospitality is a gospel imperative, as well as a practical necessity in growing the church. It is a good sign when the coffee hour lasts as long as, if not longer than, worship itself.

- Let hospitality follow, directly and naturally, every act of worship.
- Let the invitation to the whole assembly be warm and insistent.
- Avoid any suggestion that this is for the few rather than for all.
- Serve refreshments as near as possible to the worship.
- Where there is no lobby, serve them in the worship space itself.
- Avoid serving them in a separate building.
- Make the transition from worship to hospitality as seamless as possible, indicating that hospitality is integral to the whole experience.
- Those serving hot drinks or other refreshments should see it as a ministry to others, being cheerful and friendly, and giving priority to new faces and helping the family to hold back.

PART 5

Conclusion

So if anyone is in Christ, there is a new creation: everything old has passed away; see, everything has become new![114]

As I said at the beginning of the book, worship is a funny paradoxical business, capable of transporting us to the gate of heaven, or driving us to distraction, even to despair. In extreme cases our experience of worship may even be the cause of our losing hope in the Church's continuing ability to proclaim and to be good news, or to pay the price of the process of continual renewal which is inseparable from that proclamation.

The sections above have attempted to identify some of the chief characteristics of good worship. While accepting that to produce worship that engages, inspires and transforms will remain a somewhat elusive goal, not suitable for bottling or encapsulating, nevertheless it is a far from unattainable one.

Good worship requires a faithful pastor on fire with the conviction that worship can change lives and situations. It requires a team of people, gathered around the pastor, who will joyfully share the task of creating worship of power and beauty. It requires an assembly ready to

---

114 2 Corinthians 5.17.

explore and experiment and to engage with a will in the sheer hard work of researching new material, redesigning the room, planning, preparing, practising, being taught (and sometimes re-taught), and aiming at the very best.

Good worship is worship which is *conscious* of its impact, aware of its potential for changing lives, mindful at every stage of the spiritual significance of every word and action. In good worship nothing is lost, or insignificant. Every crumb we let fall is gathered up in the divine economy to be reshaped into bread that will give life.

Let no one underestimate the task, or the degree of upheaval that will flow inevitably from any serious attempt to transform worship. No amount of tweaking the existing order – a new hymn here, a front pew removed there – will achieve anything very much. So immured are we in patterns of worship from a bygone era, that to break free will be a costly, though exhilarating, process.

A complete refurbishment is called for, taking the structure back to its bare walls, exposing the beams, and starting again with a wholesale renewal of every component. In the best work of renovation, however, the building stands firm throughout though stripped to its bare bones. It remains recognizable and familiar, but sparkles with new life and vitality, ready for another few hundred years.

We shall need to stand back, think long and hard and courageously, and then strip our worship back to its bare essentials. Having gone through that costly process we can begin to refurbish and re-equip, clothing the structure with a fine new suit of clothes in keeping with who we are and where we are going.

Good worship enables us to see familiar things in a different light, recognizing the splendour of God in unlikely places, the potential of all things and all people. The story in Genesis[115] of Jacob's flight from his brother Esau whom he had wronged, describes how he rested for the night in 'a certain place', and how he took 'one of the stones of the place' as a pillow on which to rest his head to sleep.

In that place, Jacob received an overwhelming sense of the presence of God, described by the writer of Genesis as a dream in which God spoke with him, blessed and commissioned him. In the morning, the ordinary stone is made into an altar, and the nondescript place given a name (Bethel) which will resound through millennia of Judeo-Christian worship. Jacob exclaims, 'Surely the Lord is in this place, and I did not know it!'

So may our worship enable us to see with fresh eyes and open hearts and clear minds the wondrous things of God made visible and tangible amid ordinary things and nondescript places. May we wake from our slumber to see, as if for the first time, everything around us irradiated by the splendour of God's presence.

Above all, may we see with fresh eyes the assembly transfigured, energized and made new, and recognize that when we come together to offer worship, no matter how ordinary the people or nondescript the surroundings, in fact we are caught up by the Spirit of God to stand on holy ground and at heaven's gate.

---

115 Genesis 28.10–22.

References and Further Reading

Book of Common Prayer 1979, Church Publishing, New York.

Barbara Brown Taylor, *When God is Silent*, Cowley, 1998.

Stephen Burns, *The SCM Study Guide to Liturgy*, SCM Press, 2008.

R.F. Buxton, *A New Dictionary of Liturgy and Worship*, SCM Press, 1986.

John le Carré, *The Looking Glass War*, **Heinemann, 1965**.

Godfried Danneels, 'Liturgy Forty Years After the Second Vatican Council', in Keith Pecklers (ed.), *Liturgy in a Postmodern World*, Continuum, 2003.

Robert Walter Funk and Roy W. Hoover (eds), *The Five Gospels*, Polebridge Press, 1993.

Richard Giles, *Re-Pitching the Tent*, Canterbury Press, 1997.

Dag Hammarskjold, *Markings*, Faber, 1972.

Selina Hastings, *The Secret Lives of Somerset Maugham*, John Murray, 2009.

Marty Haugen, 'Here in this Place' © GIA Publications, Inc, 1982.

Robert Hovda, *Strong, Loving and Wise: Presiding in Liturgy*, Liturgical Press, 1976.

Christopher Irvine, *The Use of Symbols in Worship*, SPCK, 2007.

Paul Janowiak, *The Holy Preaching*, Liturgical Press, 2000.

Aidan Kavanagah, *Elements of Rite*, Liturgical Press, 1990.

Dirk Lange and Dwight Vogel (eds), *Ordo: Bath, Word, Prayer, Table*, OSL Publications, 2005.

John K. Leonard and Nathan D. Mitchell, *Postures of the Assembly during the Eucharistic Prayer*, Liturgy Training Publications, 1994.

C.S. Lewis, *The Lion, the Witch and the Wardrobe: The Chronicles of Narnia*, HarperCollins, 2009.

Michael Marshall, *Renewal in Worship*, Marshall, Morgan & Scott, 1982.

Ferdinand Mount, *Cold Cream: My Early Life and Other Mistakes*, Bloomsbury, 2008.

Hugh Muir, *Guardian Diary*, 15 June 2010.

Keith Pecklers, *Liturgy in a Postmodern World*, Continuum, 2003.

Catherine Pickstock, *After Writing: On The Liturgical Consummation of Philosophy*, Wiley-Blackwell, 1997.

Gerard Pottebaum, *The Rites of People*, Pastoral Press, 1992.

John Potter and Evelyn Simpson (eds), *The Sermons of John Donne*, Vol. 9, Berkeley, 1953–62.

Timothy Radcliffe, in Keith Pecklers (ed.), *Liturgy in a Post-Modern World*, Continuum, 2003.

Thich Nhat Hanh, *Living Buddha, Living Christ*, Riverhead Trade, 1997.

Catherine Vincie, *Celebrating Divine Mystery*, Liturgical Press, 2009.

Cyrille Vogel, *Liturgy: Self Expression of the Church*, Concilium, 1972.

Kallistos Ware, *The Orthodox Church*, Pelican, 1995.